RESCUING KNOWLEDGE PROJECT
A CAGLIASTRO ENDEAVOR

DEVIL WORSHIP; THE SACRED BOOKS AND TRADITIONS OF THE YEZIDIZ

by Isya Joseph, Originally Published 1919

Original Publisher Boston, R. G. Badger Gorham Press

EXPANDED WITH BLANK PAGES FOR NOTES AND DATA

Forward, structure and comments by

THE

SORCERESS CAGLIASTRO

RESCUING KNOWLEDGE PROJECT

A CAGLIASTRO ENDEAVOR

NORTH SEA TALES PUBLISHING

FORWARD TO THE NEW PRINTING, BY CAGLIASTRO

The Yezidis....the misnomer of "Devil Worship....?"

"When you kill someone, you kill yourself" **Yezidi Faqi**

Who Are the Yezidis?

The following quote is from the home page of www.yeziditruth.org

"The Yezidis or Yazidis are a Kurdish speaking people who live principally in northern Iraq. They number approximately 800,000. They are mostly a poor and oppressed people, but they have a rich spiritual tradition that they contend is the world's oldest. They were the first people to be created in the Garden of Eden, which they claim is a large area centered in what is now known as Lalish in Iraq."

I am including that opening here because I am of the opinion that there is a powerful underlying connection between the unquenchable desire for horrific destruction of these people and their antiquities - and the overwhelming desire for extremists to control humanity through a force which few know. I may or may not have the correct point of view here – however I am a professional at reading sensations, as is my group, THE FIRM. On more than one occasion we have found ourselves back at the starting point of the Yezidi's as the power seat of the control of entities that are held in situ amongst their powerful elders.

I am a Necromancer, and one who works with Daemons. I am not an anthropologist or a physicist... I mention that as that is crucial to the understanding of what it is I am presenting herein, as well as to leave a train of crumbs to the core reason for which I am presenting this work, this RESCUED KNOWLEDGE BOOK..

DEVIL WORSHIP; THE SACRED BOOKS AND TRADITIONS OF THE YEZIDIZ

printed in 1919

The BOOK itself that is within this new publication was written in 1919 and it is important for the reader to remember that they are reading a text which is, at this writing, only a few years shy of being a century old.

To my point I feel that the Yezidi sit upon a secreted entity, force, a controlled power... Note the following... On page numbered eleven in the introduction of the book contained herein, the author writes that he was in the presence of a particular family member of "the only Yezidi family who could read and guard the sacred tradition of the sect.", texts, some of which date back to the twelfth century.

Their numbers vary which I feel lends to the mystery regarding their true mission....

On page thirteen of the forward in this 1919 publication, the author states "The Yezidis, frequently called "Devil-Worshippers," are a small and obscure religious sect, numbering about 200,000. They are scattered over a belt of territory three hundred miles wide, extending in length from the neighborhood of Aleppo in northern Syria to the Caucasus in southern Russia."

The website www.yeziditruth.org states:

Even with all of their ostensible connections to other faiths, the Yezidis have for hundreds of years been under constant attack from Moslems who promulgate the idea that the Yezidi's principle deity, Tawsy Melek, the "Peacock Angel", is Satan. Moslems also contend that the Yezidis are not "People of the Book", i.e., that they don't have a sacred revealed scripture like the Holy Bible or the Koran at the center of their religion, so they claim justification in their massacre of them.

Or even worse, some Moslems have pronounced the Yezidis as heretics who were once orthodox Moslems – an allegation that puts them in the lowest rung of humanity. Over the course of 700 years, nearly 23 million Yezidi people have been murdered, thus bringing their civilization to the brink of extinction.

Wikipedia states: "The bulk of the Yazidi population lives in Iraq, where they make up an important minority community. Estimates of the size of these communities vary significantly, between 70,000 and 500,000. They are particularly concentrated in northern Iraq in the Nineveh Province. The two biggest communities are in Shekhan, northeast of Mosul, and in Sinjar, at the Syrian border 80 kilometres (50 mi) west of Mosul. In Shekhan is the shrine of Sheikh Adi ibn Musafir at Lalish. During the 20th century, the Shekhan community struggled for dominance with the more conservative Sinjar community. The demographic profile has probably changed considerably since the beginning of the Iraq War in 2003 and the fall of Saddam Hussein's regime."

The truth about their beliefs are complex, and of course, like all emotional subjects, are explained from the slant of the writer's beliefs. However, THIS WRITER has no beliefs, as those of you are familiar with my work already know. So, that being said, I will share with the reader what I understand to be the nuts and bolts of the belief structure held by the Yezidis.

The Yazidis are:

+Monotheist adhering to the belief in one god as creator of the world

+The world was placed by this one god under the care of seven holy beings or angels

+Melek Taus, the Peacock Angel is the chief who, as world-ruler, causes both good and bad to befall individuals

+Melek Taus, is thought to have an ambivalent character which is reflected in the myths of his own temporary fall from the one god's favor, before his remorseful tears extinguished the fires of his hellish prison and he was reconciled with the one god

Wikipedia says:

IMPORTANT NOTE TO THE READER – these are WIKIPEDIA's statements which I place here only to illustrate the connection of the term DEVIL WORSHIP to the Yezidi. This statement does NOT reflect my own thoughts on the entity known as Satan.

“”This belief builds on Sufi mystical reflections on Iblis, who refused to prostrate to Adam despite God's express command to do so. **Because of this connection to the Sufi Iblis tradition, some followers of other monotheistic religions of the region equate the Peacock Angel with their own unredeemed evil spirit Satan which has incited centuries of persecution of the Yazidis as "devil worshippers."** Persecution of Yazidis has continued in their home communities within the borders of modern Iraq, under fundamentalist Sunni Muslim revolutionaries.

Starting in August 2014, the Yazidis were targeted by the Islamic State of Iraq and the

Levant in its campaign to "purify" Iraq and neighboring countries of non-Islamic influences.""

The truth, if one perceives the truth as that which is told directly from the mouths of the people involved and which they perceive as fact, is that the origin of the Yezidi religion is rooted in the story of the Prophet Noah and the placement of the animals into the ark. The Yezidi believe that there was a hole in the bottom of the boat and that Noah asked a black snake to place himself in the hole so the boat would not sink. The Yezidi people must respect the black snake because it saved humanity by this task. Thusly there is a black snake painted inside the door of the main temple on Yezidi ground, and even outside of other temples....

After this incident the one god restored the earth and sky and there were seven angles. Six obeyed this one god and one did not. That one was given the name Azazel and that angel challenged the one god stating that the one god created Adam from the soil and angels from the light. Yazidis consider themselves the direct descendants of Adam and perceive good and evil as the same faces of the same reality. They state that "choosing the right side is up to each person's soul"... – So the angel who challenged the command of Adam asked logically - how can the light obey the soil?

According to this mythology, what is more commonly told as “Lucifer”, the beautiful and vain angel of heaven, did not betray the one god and create evil, but simply manifested himself to the world, becoming the bridge between humans and the Creator. (Note, from this author’s point of view I am discussing well known mythology only).

So in order to protect themselves, the Yazidi then took the angel, who was renamed Melek Taus, and situated him so that he could be in the sky looking over all humanity. He was given the form of a peacock. Melek Taus, as the Yazidis call him, is still worshipped in the Temple of Lalish, the sect's holy site in northwestern Iraq.

This approach of focusing their worship upon what was thought to be the fallen angel has caused the Yazidi to be called Devil Worshippers for several reasons. This is enhanced by the theory which feeds off of the many stereotypes in Turkey, Syria, Iran and Iraq that as a people, the Yezidi are resistant to education for their children. It is rather, such that until recently, there were no governmental schools but plenty of religious ones so Yezidi families removed their children from religious schools in order to prevent them from being converted to Islam.

Another damaging bit of folklore which substantiates the moniker of Devil Worshipper is that the image of the peacock and its perceived vanity was considered a manifestation of the Satan's power by many ancient communities as well as followers of the old Zarathustrian faith.

This results in a furthering of applied acceptance of the stereotype of misrepresentation of the Yazidi divinity Melek Taus, the vain peacock - leading Muslims and other travelers alike to continue to perpetrate the "devil Worship" fallacy. This only inflames the myths regarding the Satan-oriented belief structure without focusing on the core of their beliefs. The Yezidi adopted a dualist approach to avoid accusations of blasphemy and Satanism. What has happened instead is that dualist approach has garnered them a level of suspicion and labeling.

Yazidis have taken aspects of Christianity and Islam and hidden in their holy place in Lalish, which is surrounded by the three mountains Arafat, Msgat and Hzrat.

ORIGIN…CHICKEN OR THE EGG?

The Yazidi people speak Kurmanji Kurdish , and although they speak mostly Kurdish, their ethnicity is obscure. Commentators identify the Yazidis as predominantly Kurds but according to some sources, they tend to regard themselves as distinct from Kurds. Many Yazidis say that Kurds are originally Yazidi who shifted culturally after they adopted Islam.

The Yezidi Name, (this passage from www.yeziditruth.org)

The Yezidis claim to have the oldest religion in the world, contending that the truth of this is reflected in the antiquity of their calendar. They can trace back their religious calendar 6756 years, thus making 2008 CE the Yezidi year of 6757. In relation to some of the other major religions, the Yezidi Calendar is 4,750 years older than the Christian or Gregorian Calendar, 990 years older than the Jewish Calender, and it is 5329 years older than the Muslim Calendar.

Since their founding many thousands of years ago in India, these people have always been known as the **Yezidis** or **Yazidis**. The term **Yezidi** or **Yazidi** is also very close to the Persion/Zoroastrian word *Yazdan*, meaning "*God*", and *Yazata*, meaning "*divine*" or "*angelic being*".

For this reason, scholars have theorized a Persian origin for the **Yezidis**. Other scholars have associated the name *Yazidi* with *Yazid bin Muawiyah*, a Moslem Caliph of the early Umayyad Dynasty. According to the current Yezidi belief, however, the Caliph Yazid was a Moslem ruler who eventually became disenchanted with his religion and converted to Yezidism.

All of this history is substantive in so much as it gives the reader an understanding of where the Yezidi fit into the history of religion, thereby touching on the most vital engine of their traditions.

How does that serve us on the investigative level regarding the reasons behind the desire to destroy the Yezidi?....

I personally have the sensation that the Yezidi are controlling a great and powerful source of energy which is subject to commands. I am a Sorceress practicing the Science of Sorcery and for me the true focus of interest is that one. Communication with Daemons and the Disincarnate are a profound aspect of my work. For an ancient, and socially speaking – powerless people - to be the point of such a desire for eradication, there must be an underlying power which would fuel the on-going desire by many to seek, and thereby force that eradication....

Food for thought...
Ancient texts for thought....a republication of
ancient texts herein....
SORCERESS CAGLIASTRO

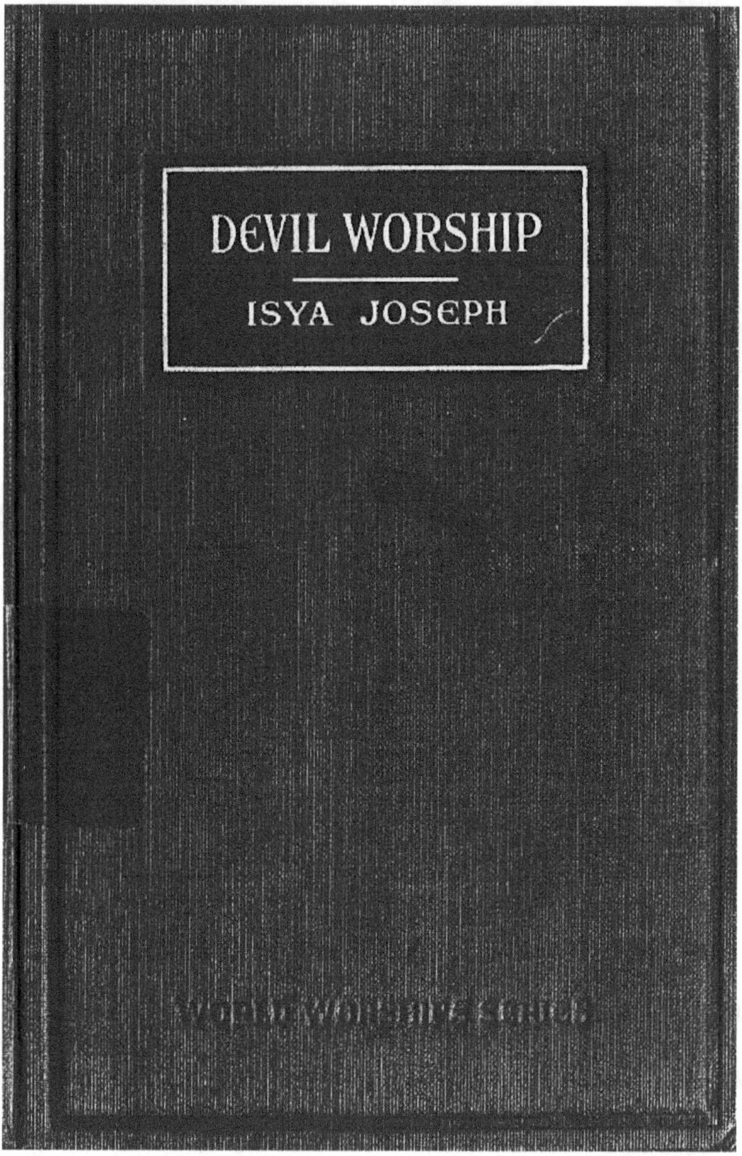
DEVIL WORSHIP
ISYA JOSEPH

THIS PAGE LEFT BLANK BY ORIGINAL PUBLISHER, USE FOR NOTES

THIS PAGE LEFT BLANK BY ORIGINAL PUBLISHER,
USE FOR NOTES

THIS PAGE LEFT BLANK BY ORIGINAL PUBLISHER, USE FOR NOTES

THIS PAGE LEFT BLANK BY ORIGINAL PUBLISHER,
USE FOR NOTES

THIS PAGE LEFT BLANK BY ORIGINAL PUBLISHER, USE FOR NOTES

THE SYMBOL OF THE DEVIL

DEVIL WORSHIP

THE SACRED BOOKS AND TRADITIONS OF THE YEZIDIZ

BY

ISYA JOSEPH, B.A., M.A., PH.D.

BOSTON

RICHARD G. BADGER

THE GORHAM PRESS

The Gorham Press, Boston, U. S. A.

Made in the United States of America

TO MY TEACHERS IN UNION THEOLOGICAL SEMINARY,
COLUMBIA, AND HARVARD UNIVERSITIES, THIS
BOOK IS INSCRIBED WITH GRATITUDE
AND ESTEEM

THIS PAGE LEFT BLANK BY ORIGINAL PUBLISHER, USE FOR NOTES

CONTENTS

CONTENTS

DEVIL WORSHIP

THIS PAGE LEFT BLANK BY ORIGINAL PUBLISHER,
USE FOR NOTES

INTRODUCTION

THE ORIGIN OF THE MANUSCRIPT

The Arabic manuscript here translated was presented to me before I left Mosul by my friend Dâud aṣ-Ṣâiġ as a memento of our friendship. Ḫawâja aṣ-Ṣâiġ was a man of culture, in sympathy with western thought, and an intimate acquaintance of M. N. Siouffi, the vice-consul of the French Republic in Mosul. From the first page of the manuscript it appears that through some Yezidis he had access to their literature. I know he was in close touch with many of them, especially with the family of Mulla Ḥaidar, which is the only Yezidi family that can read and guard the sacred tradition of the sect.

The manuscript comprises a brief Introduction, the Sacred Books, and an Appendix. In the first, the compiler indicates the sources of his information and gives a sketch of the life of Šeiḫ 'Adî, the chief saint of the Yezidis.

The Sacred Books comprise *Kitâb al- Jilwah* (Book of Revelation), and *Maṣḥaf Rêš* (Black Book)—so named because in it mention is made of the descent of the Lord upon the Black Mountain (p. 32). *Al Jilwah*[1] is ascribed to Šeiḫ 'Adî himself, and would accordingly date from the twelfth century A. D. It is divided into a brief introduction and five short chapters. In each, 'Adî is represented as the speaker. In the Preface the Šeiḫ says that he existed with Melek Tâ'ûs before the creation of the world, and that he was sent by his god Tâ'ûs to instruct the Yezidi sect in truth. In the first chapter he asserts his omnipresence and omnipotence; in the second he claims to have power to reward those who obey him and to punish those who disobey him; in the third he declares that he possesses the treasures of the earth; in the fourth he warns his followers of the doctrines of those that are without; and in the fifth he bids them keep his commandments and obey his servants, who will communicate to them his teachings. The *Black Book*,[2] which perhaps dates from the thirteenth century, is larger than the Book of Revelation, but is not divided into chapters. It begins with the narrative of creation: God finishes his work in seven days—Sunday to Saturday. In each day he creates an angel or king (*melek*). Melek Ṭâ'ûs, who is created on Sunday, is made chief of all. After that Fahr-ad Dîn creates the planets, man, and animals. Then follows a story about Adam and Eve, their temptation and quarrel; the coming of the chief angels to the world to establish the Yezidi kingdom; the flood; the miraculous birth of Yezîd bn Mu'awiya; and certain ordinances in regard to food, the New Year, and marriages.

The Appendix contains the following:

1. A collection of materials concerning the Yezidi belief and practice.
2. A poem in praise of Šeiḫ 'Adî.
3. The principal prayer of the Yezidis, in the Kurdish language.
4. A description of the Yezidi sacerdotal system.
5. A petition to the Ottoman government to exempt the sect from military service, presented in the year 1872 A. D.

An analysis of the texts shows that the material is taken from different sources: part of it is clearly derived from the religious books of the sect; another part from a description of the beliefs and customs of the sect given by a member of it to an outsider; a third, partly from observations by an outsider, partly from stories about Yezidis current among their Christian neighbors. Unfortunately the compiler does not specify whence each particular part of his information is obtained. On closer examination it is evident that part, at least, of the Arabic in hand is a translation from Syriac.

The Yezidis, frequently called "Devil-Worshippers," are a small and obscure religious sect, numbering about 200,000.[3] They are scattered over a belt of territory three hundred miles wide, extending in length from the neighborhood of Aleppo in northern Syria to the Caucasus in southern Russia. The mass of them, however, are to be found in the mountains of northern and central Kurdistan and among the Sinjar Hills of Northern Mesopotamia.

By reason of their mysterious religion, the Devil-Worshipers have been an object of interest and investigation for several generations. Our chief first-hand sources of information in regard to the manners, customs, and practices of these people are: Sir Henry Layard, *Nineveh and its Remains* (1849), *Nineveh and Babylon* (1853); G. P. Badger, *The Nestorians and their Rituals* (1852); my honored teacher, Rev. A. N. Andrus, veteran missionary of the A. B. C. F. M., resident in Mardin, Mesopotamia, "The Yezidis," in the *Encyclopaedia of Missions;* P. Anastase, "The Yezidis," in the Arabic periodical, *Al-Mašrik,* Vol. II (1899); Professor A. V. Williams Jackson, of Columbia University, *Persia Past and Present* (1906); "The Yezidis," in the *International Encyclopaedia, s. v.;* also in *JAOS*, XXV, 178; M. N. Siouffi, in the *Journal Asiatique,* 1882 (viie série, T. 20), p. 252, and 1885 (viiie série, T. 5), p. 78. Siouffi was the first to discover and establish the historical character of Šeiḫ 'Adî, about whom the scholars had been puzzled. He published an extract relating to 'Adî from Ibn Ḫallikân's *Wafaiyât 'al-Ayân* (bibliographical work). Of the second-hand sources of information may be mentioned *Les Yezidis,* by J. Menant (Paris, 1892), and the article by Victor Dingelstedt, "The Yezidis," in the *Scottish Geographical Magazine,* Vol. XIV, pp. 259 ff.[4]

In addition to these descriptions, several manuscripts have come to light of recent years which give a great deal of information about the beliefs and customs of the Yezidis

Two of these manuscripts are in the Bibliothèque Nationale, in Paris (*Fond Syriaque*, Nos. 306 and 325). A translation of the Arabic (Carshuni) texts in these manuscripts relative to the Yezidis was published by Professor E. H. Browne in an appendix to O. H. Parry, *Six Months in a Syrian Monastery*, 1895. Professor Browne at that time proposed to edit the Arabic text (see J.-B. Chabot, *Journal Asiatique*, 1896, ixe série, T. 7, p. 100); but so far as I can ascertain this intention has not been carried out.

The manuscript translated by Browne, which according to Parry (*loc. cit.*, p. 357) was written by a native of Mosul, seems to be closely related to that translated below. There are, however, some differences in contents and arrangement: my copy is divided into the Book of Revelation, the Black Book, and an Appendix; while Browne's embraces the Book of Revelation which corresponds to that in my manuscript), and two other "Accounts," the greater part of which is contained in the Black Book of my text, and the rest in the Appendix. Further, in my manuscript *Al-Jilwah* immediately follows the Introduction; while in Browne's the discussion of the sacerdotal system, the petition to the Ottoman government, and some other matters, are inserted between the Introduction and *Al-Jilwah*. In Browne's, moreover, the

Poem in Praise of Šeiḫ 'Adî, and the Principal Prayer (in Kurdish) are absent, while the petition to the Turkish government is briefer, and lacks articles iv and xiv. The text of this petition, in its original form, was published by Lidzbarski in *ZDMG*, LI, 592 ff., after a manuscript in Berlin which was procured from Šammas Eremia Šamir.

Two Syriac texts have also been printed. The first, edited and translated by J.-B. Chabot in the *Journal Asiatique*, 1896 (ixᵉ série, T. 7), p. 100 ff., from the Paris manuscripts referred to above, corresponds, with slight variations, to the second "Account," of Browne (Parry, *loc. cit.*, pp. 380-87).

The second was published with an Italian translation, by Samuel Giamil, under the title, *Monte Singar; Storia di un Popolo Ignoto* (Rome, 1900), from a manuscript copied for him in 1899 from an original in the monastery of Rabban Hormizd. The author of this work, a Syrian priest, Isaac, lived for a long time among the Yezidis, and not only had unusual opportunities of observation, but, as is evident from several anecdotes, possessed their confidence and esteem in a singular degree. His work is in catechetical form: a youthful Yezidi inquirer questions a teacher about the beliefs, traditions, and customs of his people, and the answers contain the fullest exposition of these matters we at present possess. Occasionally the author falls out of his role, and lets it appear that the questioner is no other than Priest Isaac himself.

The work is divided into ten sections, which treat

respectively of the works of God and his abode (p.3); the creation of Adam and Eve (p. 8); the wonderful deeds of the god Yezîd (p. 16); the Yezidi saints (p. 27); the New-Year (p. 32); marriage customs (p. 46); death and burial (p. 53); the pilgrimage to Šeiḫ 'Adî's shrine (p. 67); the festivals and assemblies at Šeiḫ 'Adî (p. 80); and the Yezidi kings (p. 87).

Apart from the *Kitâb al-Jilwah,* Priest Isaac's work is clearly the source from which is derived most of the material in the Syriac and Arabic manuscripts that have hitherto come to light.

Beside the Arabic manuscript from Dâud aṣ-Ṣâiġ which is translated below, I have in my possession two others, which were sent me by the Rev. A. N. Andrus. The first of these written by Šammas Eremia Šamir (designated in the notes hereafter as SS), seems to be a duplicate of that from which Browne's translation was made. They agree in contents and arrangement, and in certain readings in which they differ from the other texts. At the close of SS the writer says that he compiled it (chiefly from *Al-Jilwah*) for the benefit of some of his friends who wished to acquaint themselves with the Yezidi religion.

The origin of the Yezidi sect has been the subject of much discussion, but no satisfactory solution of the problem has as yet been reached. There are those who assert that the Yezidis are the remains of the ancient Manichaeans;[3] others entertain the view that the Yezidis were originally Christians, whom progressive ignorance has brought into their present condition[6]—some even going so far as to connect the name "Yezidi" with "Jesus"![7] Some think that the Yezidi sect takes its name from the Persian word *yazd*, 'god, or good spirit,' over against Ahriman, the evil principle;[8] while others associate it with *Yazd* or *Yezid*, a town in central Persia, the inhabitants of which are chiefly Parsees.[9] Some finally maintain that the sect was founded by Šeiḫ 'Adî.[10]

The Yezidis themselves had a curious legend connecting the name with the Caliph Yezîd bn Mu'âwiya[11] (see p. 37).

In a dissertation presented for the degree of Doctor of Philosophy in Harvard University I called attention to a statement of aš-Šahrastânî the importance of which seems hitherto not to have been appreciated, but which appears to me to give the most probable explanation of the name and of the original affinities of the sect. The passage is as follows (*Kitâb al Milal wan-Nihal*, ed. Cureton, I, 101):

The Yezidis are the followers of Yezîd bn Unaisa, who kept friendship with the first Muhakkama, before the Azariḳa; he separated himself from those who followed after them with the exception of the Abadiyah,[12] for with these he kept friendly. He believed that God would send an apostle from among the Persians, and would reveal to him a book that is already written in heaven, and would reveal the whole (book) to him at one time,[13] and as a result he would leave the religion of Mohammed, the Chosen One—

may God bless and save him!—and follow the religion of the Sabians mentioned in the Koran.[14] (These are not the Sabians who are found in Ḥarân and Wasit.[15]) But Yezîd associated himself with the people of the Book who recognized the Chosen One as a prophet, even though they did not accept his (Mohammed's) religion. And he said that the followers of the ordinances are among those who agree with him; but that others are hiding the truth and give companions to God, and that every sin, small or great, is idolatry.[16]

The statement of Aš-Šahrastânî is so clear that it can bear no other interpretation than that the Yezidis were the followers of Yezîd bn Unaisa. He calls them his *'aṣḥâb,* that is, his followers, a term by which he designates the relation between a sect and its founder.[17] The statement comes from the pen of one who is considered of the highest authority among the Arab scholars on questions relating to philosophical and religious sects.[18] This precise definition of the position of Yezîd bn Unaisa in the sectarian conflicts of the first century of Islam seems to show that he had exact information about him.

The prediction about the Persian prophet is quoted, almost in the same words, by another great Mohammedan authority on religious sects, Ibn Ḥazm, who lived a century before Aš-Šahrastânî. (The Egyptian edition of Ibn Ḥazm, Vol. IV, p. 188, reads Zaid bn Abi *Ubaisa;* but that Unaisa should be restored is evident from the fact that Ibn Ḥazm is at pains to distinguish the author of this unorthodox prediction from the well-known traditionist of the name—e. g., Tabari, I, 135.[19]

The prophecy was perhaps preserved among the leaders of the Abaḍiya, with which sect Yezîd bn Unaisa is associated. Aš-Šahrastânî's statement, the significant part of which we have found also in Ibn Ḥazm was doubtless derived from an older written source.

Who is intended by the coming Persian prophet—if, indeed, any particular individual is meant—it is not possible to determine. Kremer[20] cannot be right in identifying him with Šeiḫ 'Adî, for the supposed prediction was in circulation a century or more before his time. He is said to have been, not a Persian, but a Syrian from Baalbek or elsewhere in the West; and both in Arabic authors[21] and in his own writings[22] he appears as a Moslem, a Sufi saint in good standing. The Yezidis to this day await the appearance of the Persian prophet.[23]

On the basis of these scanty bits of fact, it appears that: The Yezidis were originally a Ḫarijite[24] subsect, akin to the Abadiya, bearing the name of their founder, Yezîd bn Unaisa. Certain distinctive Ḫarijite peculiarities seem indeed to have outlived among them the common faith of Islam; such as the tolerant judgment of Jews and Christians; the condemnation of every sin as implicit idolatry. In their new seats in Kurdistan, whither they migrated about the end of the fourteenth century[25] they were drawn into the movement of which Šeiḫ 'Adî was in his life time the leader and after his death the saint, and ended by making of him the incarnation of God in the present age.[26] With this they joined elements drawn from Christianity,[27] with here and there a trace of Judaism, and with large survivals of the persistent old Semitic heathenism, many of which they share with their neighbors of all creeds.

Difficult problems,[28] however, remain unsolved, especially the origin and nature of the worship of Melek Ṭâ'ûs.[29] The certain thing is that the actual religion of the Yezidis is a syncretism, to which Moslem, Christian (heretical, rather than orthodox), pagan, and perhaps also Persian religions have contributed.[30]

NOTES ON THE INTRODUCTION

[1] Al-Jilwah is said to have been written in 558 A. H., by Šeiḫ Faḫr-ad-Dîn, the secretary of Šeiḫ 'Adî, at the dictation of the latter. The original copy, wrapped in linen and silk wrappings, is kept in the house of Mulla Haidar, of Baadrie. Twice a year the book is taken to Šeiḫ 'Adî's shrine. (Letter from Šammas Jeremia Šamir to Mr. A. N. Andrus, of Mardin, dated October 28, 1892.)

[2] The Black Book is said to have been written by a certain Ḥasan al-Baṣrî, in 743 A. H. The original copy is kept in the house of Kehyah (chief) 'Alî, of Kasr 'Az-ad-Dîn, one hour west of Semale, a village east of Tigris. The book rests upon a throne, having over it a thin covering of red broadcloth, of linen, and other wrappings. Then is disclosed the binding, which is of wood.

[3] The exact number of the Yezidis is unknown See also Société de Géographie de l'Est, *Bulletin*, 1903, p. 284; Al Mašriḳ, II, 834.

[4] For a fuller account of the literature on the Yezidis, consult J. Menant, *Les Yézidis*, and Paul Perdrizet, Société de Géographie de l'Est, *Bulletin*, 1903, pp. 281 ff.

[5] Société de Géographie de l'Est, *Bulletin*, 1903, p. 297.

[6] Fraser, *Mesopotamia and Persia*, pp. 285, 287; Rich, *Residence in Kurdistan*, II, 69; *Al Mašriḳ*, II, 396; Badger, *The Nestorians and their Rituals*, I, 111; Assemani, *Bibliotheca Orientalis*, III, 439.

[7] Michel Febvre, *Theatre de la Turquie*, p. 364; Société de Géographie de l'Est, *Bulletin*, 1903, pp. 299, 301; cf. also J. Menant, *Les Yézidis*, pp. 52, 86, 132.

[8] Oppenheim, *Vom Mittelmeer zum persischen Golf*, 1900, II, 148; Victor Dingelstedt, *Scottish Geographical Magazine*, XIV, 295; Southgate, *A Tour through Armenia*, II, 317; A. V. Williams Jackson, "Yezidis," in the *New International Encyclopedia*, XVII, 939; Perdrizet, loc. cit., p. 299.

[9] A. V. Williams Jackson, *Persia Past and Present*, p. 10, *New International Encyclopedia*, "Yezidis;" Perdrizet, loc. cit.

[10] Dingelstedt, loc. cit.; *Revue de l'Orient Chrétien*, I, "Kurdistan."

[11] Société de Géographie de l'Est, loc. cit.; *Encyclopedia of Missions*, "Yezidis"; A. V. Williams Jackson, loc. cit.

[12] On these sects consult Aš-Šahrastânî, I, 86, 89, 100.

[13] Not like Mohammed, to whom, according to Moslem belief, the Koran was revealed at intervals.

[14] On the Ṣabians of the Koran, see Baiḍâwi and Zamaḫšari on *Suras* 2, 59; 5, 73; 22, 17.

[15] On the Ṣabians of Harrân, see Fihrist, p. 190; on the Ṣabians in general consult Aš-Šahrastânî, II, 203; on the location of Ḥarrân and Wasit, see Yaḳût, II, 331, and IV, 881.

[16] To get more particular information in regard to Yezîd bn Unaisa, I wrote to Mosul, Bagdad, and Cairo, the three centers of Mohammedan learning, and strange to say, none could throw any light on the subject.

[17] Al-Haraṯiyah he describes as *Aṣḥâb Al-Ḥareṯ* (I, 101), al-Ḥafaziyah, Aṣḥâb Ḥafez (*ibid.*), etc.

[18] Ibn Hallikân says: "Aš-Šahrastânî, a dogmatic theologian of the Ašarite sect, was distinguished as an Imâm and a doctor of the law. He displayed the highest abilities as a jurisconsult. The *Kitâb al-Milal wa-n-Nihal* (this is the book in which Aš-Šahrastânî traces the Yezidi sect to Yezîd bn Unaisa) is one of his works on scholastic theology. He remained without an equal in that branch of science."

[19] It is to be noticed also that the name "Unaisa" is very common among the Arabs; cf. Ibn Sa'ad (ed. Sachau), III, 254, 260, 264, 265, 281, 283, 287, 289; Musnad, VI, 434; Mishkat, 22, 724.

[20] *Geschichte der herrschenden Ideen des Islams*, p. 195.

[21] Ibn Hallikân (Egyptian edit., A. H. 1310), I, 316; Mohammed al-'Omari, al-Mausili, "Šeih 'Adî," quoted by M. N. Siouffi, *Journal asiatique*, 1885, 80; Yakut, IV, 374.

[22] 'Itikad Ahl as-Sunna, "Belief of the Sunnites," the Waṣaya, "Counsels to the Califs"; cf. C. Huart, *History of Arabic Literature*, p. 273.

[23] See p. 61 of this book.

[24] Aš-Šahrastânî regards them a Harijîte sub-sect.

[25] Layard, *Nineveh and its Remains*, II, 254.

[26] Mohammed al-'Omari al-Mausili and Yâsîn al-Hâtib al-'Omari al-Mausili, "Šeih 'Adî," quoted by M. N. Siouffi, *Journal asiatique*, Série viii, V (1885), 80.

[27] George Warda, Bishop of Arbila, *Poems*, edited by Heinrich Hilgenfeld, Leipzig, 1904.

[28] Such as their ceremonies at Šeih 'Adî (Badger, *The Nestorians*, I, 117), which have obtained for them the name Cherağ Sonderan, "The Extinguishers of Light." Bar Hebraeus (*Chronicon Eccles.*, ed. Abeloos-Lamy, I, 219) speaks of similar practices

among what he calls "Borborians," a branch of the Manichaeans, and calls them "The Extinguishers of Light." This name is applied to other eastern sects also; see *Abhandlungen für die Kunde des Morgenlandes*, V, 124.

[29] Professor Jackson, of Columbia University, seems to trace it to the "old devil-worship in Mazanderan" (*JAOS*, XXV, 178). But it is not certain that the Yezidis believe in Melek Ṭâ'ûs as an evil spirit. In the history of religion the god of one people is the devil of another. Asura is a deity in the Rig Veda and an evil spirit only in later Brahman theology. In Islam the gods of heathenism are degraded into jinns, just as the gods of North Semitic heathenism are called še'irîm (hairy demons) in Lev. 17:7; or as the gods of Greece and Rome became devils to early Christians. See W. R. Smith, *Religion of the Semites*, p. 120; Fihrist, pp. 322, 326.

Professor M. Lidzbarski (*ZDMG*, LI, 592), on the other hand, argues that Ṭâ'ûs is the god Tammuz. His contention is based on the assumption that the word Ṭâ'ûs must embody the ancient god; that in Fihrist, 322, the god Tâuz has a feast on the 15th of Tammuz (July); that in Kurdish, the language of the Yezidis, *m* is frequently changed to *w*. This theory also is untenable, for one might guess at any ancient god. The exact form of the name "Tauz" is uncertain (see Chwolsohn, *Die Ssabier*, II, 202; the statement that in Kurdish *m* is frequently changed to *w* is not true, if one would set it up as a grammatical rule to explain such phenomena; the Kurdish-speaking people never pronounce Tammuz, "Tauz;" and, finally, in the Yezidi conception of Melek Ṭâ'ûs there are no traces of the notion held respecting Tammuz.

[80] Such a state of affairs finds a historical parallel in other religions. Take, for example, Christianity. In it we find that the distinctive characteristics of the founder have been wrapped up in many foreign elements brought in by those who came from other religions.

PART I

THE TRANSLATION OF THE ARABIC TEXT

THIS PAGE LEFT BLANK BY ORIGINAL PUBLISHER,
USE FOR NOTES

PREFACE

In the Name of the Most Compassionate God!

With the help of the Most High God, and under his direction, we write the history of the Yezidis, their doctrines, and the mysteries of their religion, as contained in their books, which reached our hand with their own knowledge and consent.

In the time of Al-Muḳtadir Billah, A. H. 295, there lived Manṣûr-al-Ḥallâj,[2] the woll-carder, and Šeiḫ 'Abd-al-Ḳâdir of Jîlân.[3] At that time, too, there appeared a man by the name of Šeiḫ 'Adî, from the mountain of Hakkari,[4] originally from the region of Aleppo or Baalbek. He came and dwelt in Mount Lališ,[5] near the city of Moṣul, about nine hours distant from it. Some say he was of the people of Ḥarrân, and related to Marwân ibn-al-Ḥakam. His full name is Šaraf ad-Dîn Abû-l-Faḍâîl, 'Adî bn Musâfir bn Ismael bn Mousa bn Marwân bn Al-Ḥasan bn Marwân. He died A. H. 558 (A. D. 1162-63). His tomb is still visited; it is near Ba'adrei, one of the villages of Moṣul, distant eleven hours. The Yezidis are the progeny of those who were the *murids* (disciples) of Šeiḫ 'Adî. Some trace their origin to Yezid,[6] others to Ḥasan-Al-Baṣrî.

AL-JILWAH (THE REVELATION)

Before all creation this revelation was with Melek Tâ'ûs, who sent 'Abd Tâ'ûs to this world that he might separate truth known to his particular people. This was done, first of all, by means of oral tradition, and afterward by means of this book, Al-Jilwah, which the outsiders may neither read nor behold.

CHAPTER I

I was, am now, and shall have no end. I exercise dominion over all creatures and over the affairs of all who are under the protection of my image. I am ever present to help all who trust in me and call upon me in time of need. There is no place in the universe that knows not my presence. I participate in all the affairs which those who are without call evil because their nature is not such as they approve. Every age has its own manager, who directs affairs according to my decrees. This office is changeable from generation to generation, that the ruler of this world and his chiefs may discharge the duties of their respective offices every one in his own turn. I allow everyone to follow the dictates of his own nature, but he that opposes me will regret it sorely. No god has a right to interfere in my affairs, and I have made it an imperative rule that everyone shall refrain from worshiping all gods. All the books of those who are without are altered by them; and they have declined from them, although they were written by the prophets and the apostles. That there are interpolations is seen in the fact that each sect endeavors to prove that the others are wrong and to destroy their books. To me truth and falsehood are known. When temptation comes, I give my covenant to him that trusts in me. Moreover, I give counsel to the skilled directors, for I have appointed them for periods that are known to me. I remember necessary affairs and execute them in due time. I teach and guide those who follow my instruction. If anyone obey me and conform to my commandments, he shall have joy, delight, and goodness.

CHAPTER II

I requite the descendants of Adam, and reward them with various rewards that I alone know. Moreover, power and dominion over all that is on earth, both that which is above and that which is beneath, are in my hand. I do not allow friendly association with other people, nor do I deprive them that are my own and that obey me of anything that is good for them. I place my affairs in the hands of those whom I have tried and who are in accord with my desires. I appear in divers manners to those who are faithful and under my command. I give and take away; I enrich and impoverish; I cause both happiness and misery. I do all this in keeping with the characteristics of each epoch. And none has a right to interfere with my management of affairs. Those who oppose me I afflict with disease; but my own shall not die like the sons of Adam that are without. None shall live in this world longer than the time set by me; and if I so desire, I send a person a second or a third time into this world or into some other by the transmigration of souls.

CHAPTER III

I lead to the straight path without a revealed book; I direct aright my beloved and my chosen ones by unseen means. All my teachings are easily applicable to all times and all conditions. I punish in another world all who do contrary to my will. Now the sons of Adam do not know the state of things that is to come. For this reason they fall into many errors. The beasts of the earth, the birds of heaven, and the fish of the sea are all under the control of my hands. All treasures and hidden things are known to me; and as I desire, I take them from one and bestow them upon another. I reveal my wonders to those who seek them, and in due time my miracles to those who receive them from me. But those who are without are my adversaries, hence they oppose me. Nor do they know that such a course is against their own interests, for might, wealth, and riches are in my hand, and I bestow them upon every worthy descendant of Adam. Thus the government of the worlds, the transition of generations, and the changes of their directors are determined by me from the beginning.

CHAPTER IV

I will not give my rights to other gods. I have allowed the creation of four substances, four times, and four corners; because they are necessary things for creatures. The books of Jews, Christians, and Moslems, as of those who are without, accept in a sense, i. e., so far as they agree with, and conform to, my statutes. Whatsoever is contrary to these they have altered; do not accept it. Three things are against me, and I hate three things. But those who keep my secrets shall receive the fulfilment of my promises. Those who suffer for my sake I will surely reward in one of the worlds. It is my desire that all my followers shall unite in a bond of unity, lest those who are without prevail against them. Now, then, all ye who have followed my commandments and my teachings, reject all the teachings and sayings of such as are without. I have not taught these teachings, nor do they proceed from me. Do not mention my name nor my attributes, lest ye regret it; for ye do not know what those who are without may do.

CHAPTER V

O ye that have believed in me, honor my symbol and my image, for they remind you of me. Observe my laws and statutes. Obey my servants and listen to whatever they may dictate to you of the hidden things. Receive that that is dictated, and do not carry it before those who are without, Jews, Christians, Moslems, and others; for they know not the nature of my teaching. Do not give them your books, lest they alter them without your knowledge. Learn by heart the greater part of them, lest they be altered.

Thus endeth the book of Al-Jilwah, which is followed by the book of Maṣḥaf Reš, i. e., the Black Book.

Mashaf Reš (The Black Book)

In the beginning God created the White Pearl out of his most precious essence. He also created a bird named Angar. He placed the White Pearl on the back of the bird, and dwelt on it for forty thousand years. On the first day, Sunday, God created Melek Anzazîl, and he is Ṭâ'ûs-Melek, the chief of all. On Monday he created Melek Dardâel, and he is Šeiḫ Ḥasan. Tuesday he created Melek Israfel, and he is Šeiḫ

Šams (ad-Dîn). Wednesday he created Melek Mihâel, and he is Šeih Abû Bakr. Thursday he created Melek Azrâel, and he is Sajad-ad-Dîn. Friday he created Melek Šemnâel, and he is Naṣir-ad-Dîn. Saturday he created Melek Nurâel, and he is Yadin (Fahr-ad-Dîn). And he made Melek Ṭâ'ûs ruler over all.*

After this God made the form of the seven heavens, the earth, the sun, and the moon. But Fahr-ad-Dîn created man and the animals, and birds and beasts. He put them all in pockets of cloth, and came out of the Pearl accompanied by the Angels. Then he shouted at the Pearl with a loud voice. Thereupon the White Pearl broke up into four pieces, and from its midst came out the water which became an ocean. The world was round, and was not divided. Then he created Gabriel and the image of the bird. He sent Gabriel to set the four corners. He also made a vessel and descended in it for thirty thousand years. After this he came and dwelt in Mount Lališ. Then he cried out at the world, and the sea became solidified and the land appeared, but it began to shake. At this time he commaned Gabriel to bring two pieces of the White Pearl; one he placed beneath the earth, the other stayed at the gate of heaven. He then placed in them the sun and the moon; and from the scattered pieces of the White Pearl he created the stars which he hung in heaven as ornaments. He also created fruit-bearing trees and plants and mountains for ornaments to the earth. He created the throne over the carpet.* Then the Great God said: "O Angels, I will create Adam and Eve; and from the essence of Adam shall proceed Šehar bn Jebr, and of him a separate community shall appear upon the earth, that of Azazîl, i. e., that of Melek Ṭâ'ûs, which is the sect of the Yezidis. Then he sent Šeiḫ 'Adî bn Musâfir from the land of Syria, and he came (and dwelt in Mount) Lališ. Then the Lord came down to the Black Mountain. Shouting, he created thirty thousand Meleks, and divided them into three divisions. They worshiped him for forty thousand years, when he delivered them to Melek Ṭâ'ûs who went up with them to heaven. At this time the Lord came down to the Holy Land (al-Ḳuds), and commanded Gabriel to bring earth from the four corners of the world, earth, air, fire, and water. He created it and put in it the spirit of his own power, and called it Adam.

Then he commanded Gabriel to escort Adam into Paradise, and to tell him that he could eat from all the trees but not of wheat.[10] Here Adam remained for a hundred years. Thereupon, Melek Ṭâ'ûs asked God how Adam could multiply and have descendants if he were forbidden to eat of the grain. God answered, "I have put the whole matter into thy hands." Thereupon Melek Ṭâ'ûs visited Adam and said "Have you eaten of the grain?" He answered, "No, God forbade me." Melek Ṭâ'ûs replied and said, "Eat of the grain and all shall go better with thee." Then Adam ate of the grain and immediately his belly was inflated. But Melek Ṭâ'ûs drove him out of the garden, and leaving him, ascended into heaven. Now

Adam was troubled because his belly was inflated, for he had no outlet. God therefore sent a bird to him which pecked at his anus and made an outlet, and Adam was relieved.

Now Gabriel was away from Adam for a hundred years. And Adam was sad and weeping. Then God commanded Gabriel to create Eve from under the left shoulder of Adam. Now it came to pass, after the creation of Eve and of all the animals, that Adam and Eve quarreled over the question whether the human race should be descended from him or her, for each wished to be the sole begetter of the race. This quarrel originated in their observation of the fact that among animals both the male and the female were factors in the production of their respective species. After a long discussion Adam and Eve agreed on this: each should cast his seed into a jar, close it, and seal it with his own seal, and wait for nine months. When they opened the jars at the completion of this period, they found in Adam's jar two children, male and female. Now from these two our sect, the Yezidis, are descended. In Eve's jar they found naught but rotten worms emitting a foul odor. And God caused nipples to grow for Adam that he might suckle the children that proceeded from his jar. This is the reason why man has nipples.

After this Adam knew Eve, and she bore two children, male and female; and from these the Jews, the Christians, the Moslems, and other nations and sects are descended. But our first fathers are Šeth, Noah, and Enosh, the righteous ones, who were descended from Adam only.

It came to pass that trouble arose between a man and his wife, resulting from the denial on the part of the woman that the man was her husband. The man persisted in his claim that she was his wife. The trouble between the two was settled, however, through one of the righteous men of our sect, who decreed that at every wedding a drum and a pipe should be played as a testimony to the fact that such a man and such a woman were married legally.

Then Melek Ṭâ'ûs came down to earth for our sect (i. e., the Yezidis), the created ones, and appointed kings for us, besides the kings of ancient Assyria, Nisroch, who is Našir-ad-Dîn; Kamush, who is Melek Faḫr-ad-Dîn, and Artâmîs, who is Melek Šams-(ad-) Dîn. After this we had two kings, Šabur (Sapor) First (224-272 A. D.) and Second (309-379), who reigned one hundred and fifty years; and our amirs down to the present day have been descended from their seed. But we hated four kings.

Before Christ came into this world our religion was paganism. King Ahab was from among us. And the god of Ahab was called Beelzebub. Nowadays we call him Pir Bub. We had a king in Babylon, whose name was Baḫtnasar; another in Persia, whose name was Aḥšuraš; and still another in Constantinople, whose name was Agriḳâlus. The Jews, the Christians, the Moslems, and even the Persians, fought us; but they failed to subdue us, for in the strength of the Lord we prevailed against them. He teaches us the first and last science. And one of his teachings is:

Before heaven and earth existed, God was on the sea, as we formerly wrote you. He made himself a vessel and traveled in it in *kunsiniyat*[11] of the seas, thus enjoying himself in himself. He then created the White Pearl and ruled over it for forty years. Afterward, growing angry at the Pearl, he kicked it; and it was a great surprise to see the mountains formed out of its cry; the hills out of its wonders; the heavens out of its smoke. Then God ascended to heaven, solidified it, established it without pillars. He then spat upon the ground, and taking a pen in hand, began to write a narrative of all the creation.

In the beginning he created six gods from himself and from his light, and their creation was as one lights a light from another light. And God said, "Now I have created the heavens; let some one of you go up and create something therein." Thereupon the second god ascended and created the sun; the third, the moon; the fourth, the vault of heaven; the fifth, the *farğ* (i. e., the morning star); the sixth, paradise; the seventh, hell. We have already told you that after this they created Adam and Eve.

And know that besides the flood of Noah, there was another flood in this world. Now our sect, the Yezidis, are descended from Na'umi, an honored person, king of peace. We call him Melek Miran. The other sects are descended from Ham, who despised his father. The ship rested at a village called 'Ain Sifni,[12] distant from Mosul about five parasangs. The cause of the first flood was the mockery of those who were without, Jews, Christians, Moslems, and others descended from Adam and Eve. We, on the other hand, are descended from Adam only, as already indicated. This second flood came upon our sect, the Yezidis. As the water rose and the ship floated, it came above Mount Sinjar,[13] where it ran aground and was pierced by a rock. The serpent twisted itself like a cake and stopped the hole. Then the ship moved on and rested on Mount Judie.

Now the species of the serpent increased, and began to bite man and animal. It was finally caught and burned, and from its ashes fleas were created. From the time of the flood until now are seven thousand years. In every thousand years one of the seven gods descends to establish rules, statutes, and laws, after which he returns to his abode. While below, he sojourns with us, for we have every kind of holy places. This last time the god dwelt among us longer than any of the other gods who came before him. He confirmed the saints. He spoke in the Kurdish language. He also illuminated Mohammed, the prophet of the Ishmaelites, who had a servant named Mu'âwiya. When God saw that Mohammed was not upright before him, he afflicted him with a headache. The prophet then asked his servant to shave his head, for Mu'âwiya knew how to shave. He shaved his master in haste, and with some difficulty. As a result, he cut his head and made it bleed. Fearing that the blood might drop to the ground, Mu'âwiya licked it with his tongue. Whereupon Mohammed asked, "What are you doing, Mu'âwiya?" He replied, "I licked thy blood with my tongue, for I feared that it might drop to the ground." Then Mohammed said to him, "You have sinned, O Mu'âwiya, you shall draw a nation after you. You shall oppose my sect." Mu'âwiya answered and said, "Then I will not enter the world; I will not marry."

It came to pass that after some time God sent scorpions upon Mu'âwiya, which bit him, causing his face to break out with poison. Physicians urged him to marry lest he die. Hearing this, he consented. They brought him an old woman, eighty years of age, in order that no child might be born. Mu'âwiya knew his wife, and in the morning she appeared a woman of twenty-five, by the power of the great God. And she conceived and bore our god Yezid. But the foreign sects, ignorant of this fact, say that our god came from heaven, despised and driven out by the great God. For this reason they blaspheme him. In this they have erred. But we, the Yezidi sect, believe this not, for we know that he is one of the above-mentioned seven gods. We know the form of his person and his image. It is the form of a cock which we possess. None of us is allowed to utter his name, nor anything that resembles it, such as *šeitân* (Satan), *ḳaitân* (cord), *šar* (evil), *šat* (river), and the like. Nor do we pronounce *mal'ûn* (accursed), or *la'anat* (curse), or *na'al*[14] (horseshoe), or any word that has a similar sound. All these are forbidden us out of respect for him. So *ḫass* (lettuce) is debarred. We do not eat it, for it sounds like the name of our prophetess Ḫassiah. Fish is prohibited, in honor of Jonah the prophet. Likewise deer, for deer are the sheep of one of our prophets. The peacock is forbidden to our Šeiḫ and his disciples, for the sake of our Ṭâ'ûs. Squash also is debarred. It is forbidden to pass water while standing, or to dress up while sitting down, or to go to the toilet room, or to take a bath according to the custom of the people.[15] Whosoever does contrary to this is an infidel. Now the other sects, Jews, Christians, Moslems, and others, know not these things, because they dislike Melek Ṭâ'ûs. He, therefore, does not teach them, nor does he visit them. But he dwelt among us; he delivered to us the doctrines, the rules, and the traditions, all of which have become an inheritance, handed down from father to son. After this, Melek Ṭâ'ûs returned to heaven.

One of the seven gods made the *sanjaḳs*[16] (standards) and gave them to Solomon the wise. After his death our kings received them. And when our god, the barbarian Yezîd, was born, he received these *sanjaḳs* with great reverence, and bestowed them upon our sect. Moreover, he composed two songs in the Kurdish language to be sung before the *sanjḳas* in this language, which is the most ancient and acceptable one. The meaning of the song is this:

Hallelujah to the jealous God.

As they sing it, they march before the *sanjaks* with timbrels and pipes. These *sanjaks* remain with our emir, who sits on the throne of Yezîd. When these are sent away, the *ḳawwâls* assemble with the emir, and the great general, the šeiḫ, who is the representative of Šeiḫ Nasir-ad-Dîn, i. e., Nïsroch, god of the ancient Assyrians.[1] They visit the *sanjaks*. Then they send each *sanjaḳ* in care of a *ḳawwâl* to its own place; one to Ḥalataneye, one to Aleppo, one to Russia, and one to Sinjar. These *sanjaks* are given to four *ḳawwâls* by contract. Before they are sent, they are brought to Šeiḫ 'Adî's tomb, where they are baptized amid great singing and dancing. After this each of the contractors takes a load of dust from Šeiḫ 'Adî's tomb. He fashions it into small balls, each about the size of a gall nut, and carries them along with the *sanjaks* to give them away as blessings. When he approaches a town, he sends a crier before him to prepare the people to accept the *ḳawwâl* and his *sanjaḳ* with respect and honor. All turn out in fine clothes, carrying incense. The women shout, and all together sing joyful songs. The *ḳawwâl* is entertained by the people with whom he stops. The rest give him silver presents, everyone according to his means.

Besides these four *sanjaks*, there are three others, seven in all. These three are kept in a sacred place for purposes of healing. Two of them, however, remain with Šeiḫ 'Adî, and the third remains in the village of Baḥazanie, which is distant from Mosul about four hours. Every four months these *ḳawwâls* travel about. One of them must travel in the province of the emir. They travel in a fixed order, differing each year. Every time he goes out, the traveler must cleanse himself with water made sour with *summak* (sumac) and anoint himself with an oil. He must also light a lamp at each idol that has a chamber. This is the law that pertains to the *sanjaks*.

The first day of our new year is called the *Serṣâlie*, i. e., the beginning of a year. It falls on the Wednesday of the first week in April[18] On that day there must be meat in every family. The wealthy must slaughter a lamb or an ox; the poor must kill a chicken or something else. These should be cooked on the night, the morning of which is Wednesday, New Year's day. With the break of day the food should be blessed. On the first day of the year alms should be given at tombs where the souls of the dead lie.

Now the girls, large and small, are to gather from the fields flowers of every kind that have a reddish color. They are to make them into bundles, and, after keeping them three days, they are to hang them on the doors[19] as a sign of the baptism of the people living in the houses. In the morning all doors will be seen well decorated with red lilies. But women are to feed the poor and needy who pass by and have no food; this is to be done at the graves. But as to the *ḳawwâls*, they are to go around the tombs with timbrels, singing in the Kurdish language. For so doing they are entitled to money. On the above-mentioned day of *Serṣâlie* no instruments of joy are to be played, because God is sitting on the throne (arranging decrees for the year),[20] and commanding all the wise and the neighbors to come to him. And when he tells them that he will come down to earth with song and praise, all arise and rejoice before him and throw upon each the squash of the feast. Then God seals them with his own seal. And the great God gives a sealed decision to the god who is to come down. He, moreover, grants him power to do all things according to his own will. God prefers doing good and charity to fasting and praying. The worship of any idol, such as Seyed-ad-Dîn or Šeiḫ Šams is better than fasting. Some layman is to give a banquet to a *kôchak* after the fasting of the latter forty days, whether it be in summer or in winter. If he (the *kôchak*) says this entertainment is an alms given to the *sanjaḳ,* then he is not released from his fasting. When it comes to pass that the yearly tithe-gatherer finds that the people have not fully paid their tithes, he whips them till they become sick, and some even die. The people are to give the *kôchaks* money to fight the Roman army, and thus save the sect (Yezidis from the wrath of the man of the year.

Every Friday a load of gifts is to be brought as an offering to an idol. At that time, a servant is to call the people aloud from the roof of a *kôchak's* house, saying, it is the call of the prophet to a feast. All are to listen reverently and respectfully; and, on hearing it, every one is to kiss the ground and the stone on which he happens to lean.

It is our law that no *ḳawwâl* shall pass a razor over his face. Our law regarding marriage is that at the time of the wedding a loaf of bread shall be taken from the house of a *kôchak* and be divided between the bride and the bridegroom, each to eat one-half. They may, however, eat some dust from Šeiḫ 'Adî's tomb instead of the bread for a blessing. Marriage in the month of April is forbidden, for it is the first month of the year. This rule, however, does not apply to *ḳawwâls;* they may marry during this month. No layman is allowed to marry a *kôchak's* daughter. Everyone is to take a wife from his own class. But our emir may have for a wife any one whom he pleases to love. A layman may marry between the ages of ten and eighty; he may take for a wife one woman after another for a period of one year. On her way to the house of the bridegroom, a bride must visit the shrine of every idol she may happen to pass; even if she pass a Christian church, she must do the same. On her arrival at the bridegroom's house, he must hit her with a small stone in token of the fact that she must be under his authority. Moreover, a loaf of bread must be broken over her head as a sign to her that she must love the poor and needy. No Yezidi may sleep with his wife on the night the morning of which is Wednesday, and the night the morning of which is Friday. Whosoever does contrary to this commandment is an infidel. If a man steal the wife of his neighbor, or his own former wife, or her sister or mother, he is not obliged to give her dowry, for she is the booty of his hand. Daughters may not inherit their father's wealth. A young lady may be sold as an acre of land is sold. If she refuses to be married, then she must redeem herself by paying her father a sum of money earned by her service and the labor of her hand.

Here ends Kitâb Reš, which is followed by several stories, some of which are told secretly, some openly.

THIS PAGE LEFT BLANK BY ORIGINAL PUBLISHER,
USE FOR NOTES

APPENDIX TO PART I

THIS PAGE LEFT BLANK BY ORIGINAL PUBLISHER,
USE FOR NOTES

APPENDIX TO PART I

They say our hearts are our books, and our šeiḫs tell us everything from the second Adam until now and the future. When they notice the sun rise, they kiss the place where the rays first fall; they do the same at sunset, where its rays last fall. Likewise they kiss the spot where the moon first casts its rays and where it last casts them. They think, moreover, that by the multiplication of presents to šieḫs and idols they keep troubles and afflictions away.

There is a great difference among the *ḳôchaks,* they contradict one another. Some say, "Melek Ṭâ'ûs appears to me and reveals to me many revelations." Others say, "We appear to people in many different ways." Some believe that Christ is Šeiḫ Šams himself. They say that they have had prophets in all times; the *ḳôchaks* are the prophets. One of the *kôchaks* says in one of his prophecies: "I was in Jonah's ship, where a lot was cast in my presence. It fell on Jonah; and he was thrown into the sea, where he remained forty days and nights." Another said: "I was sitting with the great God, who said, 'I hope the time will come when I shall send Christ to the world.' I said to him, 'Yes.' Then he sent him. After making a sign in the sun, Christ came down to the earth." He appeared to our sect only, and made for us seven circles, which are at Šeiẖ 'Adî. Now he appeared to us because we observe the necessary order, which the other sects do not observe. Their origin and race are unknown; ours are known. We are emirs and sons of emirs; we are šeiẖs and sons of šeihs; we are *ḳôchaks* and sons of *ḳôchaks,* etc. But Christians and Moslems make priests and mullas for themselves out of those who had none of their kindred in those offices before, and never will have afterward. We are better than they. We are allowed to drink wine; our young men also may desire it when they, in company with women, engage in religious dancing and playing. Some of the *ḳôchaks* and šeiẖs, however, are not allowed to drink it. When one is about to die, he is visited by a *ḳôchak,* who places a bit of Šeiẖ 'Adî's dust in his mouth. Before he is buried his face is anointed with it. Moreover, the dung of sheep is placed on his tomb. Finally, food is offered on behalf of the dead. The *ḳôchaks* pray for the dead at the graves, for which service they are paid. They tell the relatives of the dead what they see in dreams and visions, and the condition of their dead, whether they have been translated to the human or to the animal race. Some people hide silver or gold coins that they plan to take out in case they are born the second time in this world. Some believe that the spirits of many righteous persons travel in the air. Those spirits make revelations to the *ḳôchaks,* who are acquainted with the world of mysteries and secrets. Life and death are in their hands.

Hence the fate of the people depends on the gratitude and honor which they show the *ḳôchaks.* According to Yezidis, hell has no existence. It was created in the time of the first Adam, they say, when our father, Ibrîḳ al-Aṣfar, was born.[21] By reason of his generosity and noble deeds, Ibrîḳ had many friends. Now, when he viewed hell he became very sad. He had a small *baḳbûḳ aṣfar,*[22] into which, as he kept weeping his tears fell. In seven years it was filled. He then cast it into hell, and all its fires were put out that mankind might not be tortured. This incident relates to one of the noble deeds of our first father, Ibrîḳ-al-Aṣfar. They have many more such upright men of noble deeds. Such an one is Mohammed Rašân, whose resting place is behind the mount of Šeiḫ Mattie.[23] He (Rašân) is exceedingly strong, so that the most sacred oaths are sworn by him. If any one becomes sick, he takes refuge in making vows to *ḫasin,* i. e., pillars of idols. Now there is a place of religious pilgrimage which is called Sitt Nafîsah. This place is a mulberry tree in the village of Ba'ašîḳa. Another such place is called 'Abdi Rašân, and is in the village of Ḳarabek. A third place of pilgrimage is in the village Baḥzanie, which is called Šeiḫ Bakû. Nearby is a spring, and beside this is a mulberry tree. Whoever is afflicted with fever, goes to that tree, hangs on its branches a piece of cloth from his clothes, and casts bread in the spring for the fish. All this he does that he may be cured. They entertain the belief that whoever unties or shakes off one of the shreds of cloth will catch the disease with which the man was afflicted when he hung it up. There are many such trees in the village of Ba'ašîḳa, and in some other places. There is also a spring of water, called in the common language 'Ain aṣ-Ṣafra (Yellow Spring). The Yezidis call it Kanî-Zarr.[24] In this swim those who are afflicted with the disease of *abû-ṣafar* (jaundice.) But those who are troubled with dropsy go for cure to the house of the Pir that lives in the village of Man Reš.

When they assemble at Šeiḫ 'Adî's, no one is allowed to cook anything. Everyone is to eat from Šeiḫ 'Adî's table. As to the *ḳôchaks*, every one of them sits on a stone, as one sits in prayer. To them the laity go, seeking succor. They give them money while making their petition, and vow to the stone on which the *ḳôchak* sits, sheep and oxen, everyone according to his means. Now, at the New Year the places are given in contract. When they assemble at the New Year, they dance and play with instruments of joy. Before eating the *kabdûš*, i.e., the vowed ox, they swim in the water of Zamzam, a spring coming from beneath the temple of Šeiḫ 'Adî. Then they eat in haste, snatching meat from the pot like fanatics, so that their hands are frequently burned. This practice is in accordance with their rules. After eating, they go up the mountain, shooting with their guns, and then return to Šeiḫ 'Adî. Everyone of them takes a little dust and preserves it for the times of wedding and death. They wear entwined girdles which they call the ties of the back (belt). They baptize these and the *sanjaḳs* with the water of Zamzam. He who is called Jawiš[25] wears a stole which is woven from the hair of a goat. It is nine spans in length and around it are *sansûls* (tinsels).

When the gathering comes to an end, they collect the money from the *ḳôchaks* and the contractors, and bring it to the emir. After everyone has taken according to his rank, the remainder goes to the emir.

They have another gathering which takes place at the feast of Al-Hijâjj. At this pilgrimage they go up to the mountain which is called Jabal al-'Arafât.[26] After remaining there an hour, they hasten toward Šeiẖ 'Adî. He who arrives there before his companions is praised much. Hence everyone tries to excel. The one who succeeds receives abundant blessings.

They still have another assembly. This is called "the road of the *ḳôchaks*," when each, putting a rope around his neck, goes up the mountain. After collecting wood they bring it to Šeiẖ 'Adî, carrying it on their backs. The wood is used for heating purposes and for the emir's cooking.

During these assemblies the *sanjaḳs* are passed around. In the first place they are washed with water made sour with sumac in order to be cleansed from their rust. The water is given away in drinks for purposes of blessing. In return money is taken. In the second place, the *kôchaks* go around with the *sanjaḳs* to collect money.

In their preaching, the šeiḫs tell the people that all kings have come from their descent, such as Nisroch,[27] who is Nasr-ad-Dîn, and Kamuš who is Faḫr-ad-Dîn, and Artâmîs, who is Šams-ad-Dîn, and many others, as Shabur and Yoram; and many royal names of the ancient kings, together with their own (Yezidi) kings, are from their seed. The sign of the Yezidi is that he wears a shirt with a round bosom. It differs from that of the other people, the bosom of whose shirts are open all the way down.

There is one occasion when no Yezidi will swear falsely, viz., when one draws a circle on the ground, and tells him that this circle belongs to Ṭâ'ûs-Melek, Šeiḫ 'Adî, and Yezîd, and *baryshabaḳei*. He places him in the middle of the circle, and then tells him that Melek Ṭâ'ûs and all those who were mentioned above will not intercede for him after his death, and that the shirt of the Jewish Nasim[29] be on his neck, and that the hand of Nasim be on his neck and eye, and that Nasim be his brother for the next world, and let him be to him for a šeiḫ and a *pir* if he does not tell the truth. Then if he swears to tell the truth, he cannot conceal anything. For an oath made under such conditions is considered greater than that made in the name of God, and even than that made in the name of one of their prophets.

They fast three days in a year from morning till evening. The fast falls in December, according to the oriental calendar. They have no prayer[30] except what is mentioned above, such as that referring to the sun.

and the moon, and asking help from šeihs and holy places when they say, "O Šeiḫ 'Adī, O Šeih Sams," and the like. They are all forbidden to teach their children anything, with the exception of two stanzas which they teach their children out of necessity and because it is traditional.

A story is told about them by reliable people. Once when Šeiḫ Naṣir was preaching in a village at Mount Sinjar, there was a Christian mason in the audience who, seeing the house filled with people, thought they were going to pray. He then pretended to take a nap, that he might amuse himself with what he should hear. He knew the kurdish language. When the Christian seemed to be asleep, but was really awake and listening, Šeiḫ Naṣir began to preach saying: "Once the great God appeared to me in vision. He was angry at Jesus because of a dispute with him. He therefore caught him and imprisoned him in a den which had no water. Before the mouth of the den he placed a great stone. Jesus remained in the den a long time, calling upon the prophets and the saints for help and asking their aid. Every one whose succor Jesus asked went to beg the great God to release him. But God did not grant their requests. Jesus therefore remained in a sorrowful state, knowing not what to do." After this the preacher remained silent for a quarter of an hour, and thus a great silence prevailed in the house. Then he went on to say: "O poor Jesus, why are you so forgotten, so neglected? Do you not know that all the prophets and all the saints have no favor with the great God unto Melek Ṭâ'ûs? Why have you forgotten him and have not called upon him?" Saying this, the preacher again remained silent as before, Afterward he again continued: "Jesus remained in the den till one day when he happened to remember Melek Ṭâ'ûs. He then sought his aid, praying, 'O Melek Ṭâ'ûs, I have been in this den for some time. I am imprisoned; I have sought the help of all the saints, and none of them coud deliver me. Now, save me from this den.' When Melek Ṭâ'ûs heard this, he descended from heaven to earth quicker than the twinkling of an eye, removed the stone from the top of the den, and said to Jesus, 'Come up, behold I have brought thee out.' Then both went up to heaven. When the great God saw Jesus, he said to him, 'O Jesus, who brought thee out of the den? Who brought thee here without my permission?' Jesus answered and said, 'Melek Ṭâ'ûs brought me out of the den and up here.' Then God said, 'Had it been another, I would have punished him, but Melek Ṭâ'ûs is much beloved by me; remain here for the sake of my honor.' So Jesus remained in heaven." The preacher added, "Notice that those who are without do not like Melek Ṭâ'ûs. Know ye that in the resurrection he will not like them either, and he will not intercede for them. But, as for us, he will put us all in a tray, carry us upon his head, and take us into heaven, while we are in the tray on his head." When the congregation heard this, they rose up, kissed his clothes and feet, and received his blessing.

Now the views of the Yezidis regarding the birth of Christ and the explanation of the name of the Apostle Peter, are found in one of their stories, which runs thus: "Verily Mary the Virgin mother of Jesus, begat Jesus in a manner unlike the rest of women. She begat him from her right side,[31] between her clothes and her body. At that time the Jews had a custom that, if a woman gave birth, all her relatives and neighbors would bring her presents. The women would call, carrying in their right hand a plate of fruits which were to be found in that season, and in the left hand they would carry a stone. This custom was a very ancient one. Therefore when Mary the Virgin gave birth to Jesus, the wife of Jonah, who is the mother of Peter, came to her; and, according to the custom, carried a plate of fruit in her right hand and a stone in her left. As she entered and gave Mary the plate, behold, the stone which was in her left hand begat a male. She called his name Simon Cifa, that is, son of the stone. Christians do not know these things as we do."

They have a story explaining the word heretic. It is this: When the great God created the heavens, he put all the keys of the treasuries and the mansions there in the hands of Melek Ṭâ'ûs, and commanded him not to open a certain mansion. But he, without the knowledge of God, opened the house and found a piece of paper on which was written. "Thou shalt worship thy God alone, and him alone shalt thou serve." He kept the paper with him and allowed no one else to know about it. Then God created an iron ring and hung it in the air between the heaven and the earth. Afterward he created Adam the first. Melek Ṭâ'ûs refused to worship Adam when God commanded him to do so. He showed the written paper which he took from the mansion and said, "See what is written here." Then the great God said, "It may be that you have opened the mansion which I forbade you to open." He answered, "Yes." Then God said to him, "You are a heretic, because you have disobeyed me and transgressed my commandment."

From this we know that God speaks in the Kurdish language, that is from the meaning of this saying, "Go into the iron ring which I, thy God, have made for whosoever does contrary to my commandment and disobeys me."

When one criticizes such a story as this by saying that God drove Melek Ṭâ'ûs from heaven and sent him to hell because of his pride before God the most high, they do not admit that such is the case. They answer: "It is possible that one of us in his anger should drive out his child from his house and let him wait until the next day before bringing him back? Of course not. Similar is the relation of the great God to Melek Ṭâ'ûs. Verily he loves him exceedingly. You do not understand the books which you read The Gospel says, 'No one ascended up to heaven but he who came down from heaven.' No one came down from heaven but Melek Ṭâ'ûs and Christ. From this we know that the great God has been reconciled to

Melek Ṭâ'ûs, who went up to heaven, just as God came down from heaven and went up again."

The following is a story told of a *kôchak*: It is related that at one time there was no rain in the village of Ba'aŝiḳa. In this village there was a Yezidi whose name was Kôchak Berû. There were also some saints and men of vision dwelling there. They (people) gathered to ask Berû to see about the rain. He told them, "Wait till tomorrow that I may see about it." They came to him on the next day and said, "What have you done concerning the question of rain? We are exceedingly alarmed by reason of its being withheld." He answered: "I went up to heaven last night and entered into the divan where the great God, Šeiḫ 'Adî, and some other šeiḫs and righteous men were sitting. The priest Isaac was sitting beside God. The great God said to me, 'What do you want, O Kôchak Berû; why have you come here?' I said to him, 'My lord, this year the rain has been withheld from us till now, and all thy servants are poor and needy. We beseech thee to send us rain as thy wont.' He remained silent and answered me not. I repeated the speech twice and thrice, beseeching him. Then I turned to the šeiḫs who sat there, asking their help and intercession. The great God answered me, 'Go away until we think it over.' I came down and do not know what took place after I descended from heaven. You may go to the priest Isaac and ask him what was said after I came down." They went to the priest and told him the story, and asked him what was said after Kôchak Berû came down. This priest Isaac was a great joker. He answered them, "After the *kôchak* came down, I begged God for rain on your behalf. It was agreed that after six or seven days he would send it." They waited accordingly, and by a strange coincidence, at the end of the period it rained like a flood for some time. Seeing this, the people believed in what they were told, and honored the priest Isaac, looking upon him as one of the saints, and thinking that he must have Yezidi blood in him. For more than twenty years this story has been told as one of the tales of their saints.

Once Šeiḫ 'Adî bn Musâfir and his *murids* were entertained by God in heaven. When they arrived, they did not find straw for their animals. Therefore Šeiḫ 'Adî ordered his *murids* to carry straw from his threshing floor on the earth. As it was being transported, some fell on the way, and has remained as a sign in heaven unto our day. It is known as the road of the straw man.

They think that prayer is in the heart; therefore they do not teach their children about it. And in their book neither is there any rule regarding prayer, nor is prayer considered a religious obligation.

Some assert that at one time Šeiḫ 'Adî, in company with Šeiḫ 'Abd-al-Ḳâdir, made a pilgrimage to Mecca, where he remained four years. After his absence Melek Ṭâ'ûs appeared to them (the two šeiḫs) in his symbol. He dictated some rules to them and taught them many things. Then he was hidden from them.

Four years later Šeiḫ 'Adî returned from Mecca; but they refused him and would not accept him. They asserted that he had died or ascended to heaven. He remained with them, but was without his former respect. When the time of his death came, Melek Ṭâ'ûs appeared to them and declared, "This is Šeiḫ 'Adî himself, honor him." Then they honored him and buried him with due veneration, and made his tomb a place of pilgrimage. In their estimation it is a more excellent spot than Mecca. Everyone is under obligation to visit it once a year at least; and, in addition to this, they give a sum of money through the šeiḫs to obtain satisfaction (that Šeiḫ 'Adî may be pleased with them). Whoever does this not is disobedient.

Moreover, it is said that the reason why the pilgrimage to his tomb is regarded as excellent by us and by God is that in the resurrection Šeiḫ 'Adî will carry in a tray all the Yezidis upon his head and take them into paradise, without requiring them to give account or answer. Therefore they regard the pilgrimage to his tomb as a religious duty greater than the pilgrimage to Mecca.

There are some domes, huts, around the tomb of Šeiḫ 'Adî. They are there for the purpose of receiving blessings from the tomb. And they are all attributed to the great Šeiḫs, as the hut of 'Abd-al-Ḳâdir-al-Jîlânî;[82] the hut of Šeiḫ Ḳadîb-al-Bân; the hut of Šeiḫ Šams-ad-Dîn; the hut of Šeiḫ Manṣûr-al-Ḥallâj, and the hut of Šeiḫ Ḥasan-al-Baṣrî. There are also some other huts. Each hut has a banner made of calico. It is a sign of conquest and victory.

Eating of deer's meat is forbidden them, they say, because the deer's eyes resemble the eyes of Šeiẖ 'Adî. Verily his virtues are well-known and his praiseworthy qualities are traditions handed down from generation to generation. He was the first to accept the Yezidi religion. He gave them the rules of the religious sect and founded the office of the ṣeiẖ. In addition to this, he was renowned for his devotion and religious exercise. From Mount Lališ, he used to hear the preaching of 'Abd-al-Ḳâdir-al-Jîlâni in Bagdad. He used to draw a circle on the ground and say to the religious ones, "Whosoever wants to hear the preaching of Al-Jîlâni, let him enter within this circle." The following custom, which we have, began with him: If we wish to swear to anyone, a ṣeiẖ draws a circle, and he who is to take an oath, enters into it.

At one time, passing by a garden, Šeiẖ 'Adî asked about lettuce; and, as no one answered, he said, "Huss" (hush). For this reason lettuce is forbidden and not eaten.

As regards fasting, they say about the month of Ramaḍân that it was dumb and deaf. Therefore, when God commanded the Moslems to fast, he likewise commanded the Yezidis, saying to them in the Kurdish language, *"sese,"* meaning "three." The Mohammedans did not understand it; they took it for *"se,"* "thirty." For this reason, they (Yezidis) fast three days. Moreover, they believe there are eating, drinking, and other earthly pleasures in the next world.[38] Some hold that the rule of heaven is in God's hands, but the rule of the earth is in Šeiḫ 'Adi's hands. Being exceedingly beloved by God, he bestowed upon him according to 'Adi's desire.

They believe in the transmigration of souls. This is evinced by the fact that when the soul of Manṣûr-al-Ḥallâj parted from his body when the Caliph of Bagdad killed him and cast his head into the water, his soul floated on the water. By a wonderful chance and a strange happening, the sister of the said Manṣûr went to fill her jar. The soul of her brother entered it. Without knowing what had happened, she came with it to the house. Being tired, she felt thirsty and drank from the jar. At that moment the soul of her brother entered her, but she did not perceive it until she became pregnant. She gave birth to a son who resembled Šeiḫ Manṣûr himself. He became her brother according to birth and her son according to imputation. The reason why they do not use drinking-vessels which have narrow mouths, or a net-like cover, is that when one drinks water from them they make a sound. When the head of Šeiḫ Manṣûr was thrown into the water it gurgled. In his honor they do not use the small jars with narrow necks.

They assert that they expect a prophet who will come from Persia to annul the law of Mohammed and abrogate Islam. They believe that there are seven gods, and that each god administers the universe for ten thousand years; and that one of these gods is

Lasiferos, the chief of the fallen angels, who bears also the name Melek Ṭâ'ûs. They make him a graven image after the form of a cock[34] and worship it. They play the tambourine and dance before it to make it rejoice with them. They (*ḳawwâls*) travel within the Yezidis' villages to collect money, at which time they take it into the houses that it may bless and honor them. Some say that Šeiḫ 'Adî is a deity; others that he is like a Vizier to God. To him all things are referred. This is Melek Ṭâ'ûs age. The ruling and administrative power is in his hands until the thousandth year. When the time comes to an end he will deliver the power to the next god to rule and administer until another thousand years shall be ended, and so on until the seventh god. And yet there is accord and love among these gods, and none is jealous of the one who may rule and administer the world for a period of ten thousand years. They have a book named Al Jilwah that they ascribe to Šeiḫ 'Adî, and they suffer no one who is not one of them to read it.

Mention is made in some of their books that the First Cause is the Supreme God, who before he created this world, was enjoying himself over the seas;[35] and in his hand was a great White Pearl, with which he was playing. Then he resolved to cast it into the sea, and when he did so this world came into being.

Moreover, they think themselves not to be of the same seed from which the rest of mankind sprung, but that they are begotten of the son of Adam, who was born to Adam of his spittle. For this reason they imagine themselves nobler and more pleasing to the gods than others.

They say they have taken fasting and sacrifice from Islam; baptism from Christians; prohibition of foods from the Jews; their way of worship from the idolaters; dissimulation of doctrine from the Rafiḍis (Shi'ites); human sacrifice and transmigration from the pre-Islamic paganism of the Arabs and from the Sabians. They say that when the spirit of man goes forth from his body, it enters into another man if it be just; but if unjust, into an animal.

THE POEM IN PRAISE OF ŠEIḪ 'ADI

Peace Be unto Him

My understanding surrounds the truth of things,
And my truth is mixed up in me,
And the truth of my descent is set forth by itself,
And when it was known it was altogether in me.
And all that are in the universe are under me,
And all the habitable parts and deserts,
And everything created is under me,
And I am the ruling power preceding all that exists.
And I am he that spoke a true saying,
And I am the just judge and the ruler of the earth.
And I am he that men worship in my glory,
Coming to me and kissing my feet.
And I am he that spread over the heavens their height.
And I am he that cried in the beginning.
And I am he that of myself revealeth all things,
And I am he to whom came the book of good tidings
From my Lord, who burneth the mountains.
And I am he to whom all created men come
In obedience to kiss my feet.
I bring forth fruit from the first juice of early youth
By my presence, and turn toward me my disciples.
And before this light the darkness of the morning
cleared away.
I guide him that asketh for guidance.
I am he that caused Adam to dwell in Paradise
And Nimrod to inhabit a hot burning fire.

And I am he that guided Aḥmed the Just,
And let him into my path and way.
And I am he unto whom all creatures
Come for my good purposes and gifts.
And I am he that visited all the heights,
And goodness and charity proceed from my mercy.
And I am he that made all hearts to fear
My purpose, and they magnify the majesty and power of my awfulness.
And I am he to whom the destroying lion came
Raging, and I shouted against him and he became stone.
And I am he to whom the serpent came,
And by my will I made him dust.
And I am he that struck the rock and made it tremble,
And made to burst from its sides the sweetest of waters.[36]
And I am he that sent down the certain truth;
For me is the book that comforteth the oppressed.
And I am he that judged justly,
And when I judged it was my right
And I am he that made the springs[36] to give water,
Sweeter and pleasanter than all waters.
And I am he that caused it to appear in my mercy,
And by my power I called it the pure.
And I am he to whom the Lord of heaven hath said,
Thou art the just Judge and Ruler of the earth.
And I am he that disclosed some of my wonders,
And some of my virtues are manifested in that which exists.
And I am he that caused the mountains to bow,
To move under me and at my will.[37]
And I am he before whose majesty the wild beasts cried;
They turned to me worshiping, and kissed my feet.
And I am 'Adî aš-Šâmî, the son of Musâfir.

Verily the All-Merciful has assigned unto me names,
The heavenly throne, and the seat, and the (seven) heavens, and the earth.
In the secret of my knowledge there is no God but me.
These things are subservient to my power.
O mine enemies, why do you deny me?
O men, deny me not, but submit.
In the day of judgment you will be happy in meeting me.
Who dies in my love, I will cast him
In the midst of Paradise, by my will and pleasure;
But he that dies unmindful of me
Will be thrown into torture in misery and affliction.
I say I am the only one and the exalted;
I create and make rich those whom I will.
Praise it to myself, for all things are by my will,
And the universe is lighted by some of my gifts.
I am the king that magnifies himself,
And all the riches of creation are at my bidding.
I have made known unto you, O people, some of my ways.
Who desireth me must forsake the world.
And I can also speak the true saying,
And the garden on high is for those who do my pleasure.
I sought the truth and became a confirming truth;
And by the like truth shall they, like myself, possess the highest place.

THE PRINCIPAL PRAYER OF THE YEZIDIS

Amen, Amen, Amen!
Through the intermediation of Šams-ad-Dîn,
Fahr ad-Dîn, Nasir-ad-Dîn,
Sajad ad-Dîn, Šeih Sin (Husein),
Šeih Bakr, Ḳâdir ar-Raḥmân.
Lord, thou art gracious, thou art merciful;
Thou art God, king of kings and lands,
King of joy and happiness,
King of good possession (eternal life).
From eternity thou art eternal.
Thou art the seat of luck (happiness) and life;
Thou art lord of grace and good luck.
Thou art king of jinns and human beings,
King of the holy men (saints),
Lord of terror and praise,
The abode of religious duty and praise,
Worthy of praise and thanks.
Lord! Protector in journeys,
Sovereign of the moon and of the darkness,
God of the sun and of the fire,
God of the great throne,
Lord of goodness.
Lord! No one knows how thou art.
Thou hast no beauty; thou hast no height.
Thou hast no going forth; thou hast no number.
Lord! Judge of kings and beggars,
Judge of society and of the world,
Thou hast revealed the repentance of Adam.
Lord, thou hast no house; thou hast no money;

Thou hast no wings, hast no feathers;
Thou hast no voice, thou hast no color.
Thou hast made us lucky and satisfied.
Thou hast created Jesus and Mary.
Lord, thou art gracious,
Merciful, faithful.
Thou art Lord; I am nothingness.
I am a fallen sinner,
A sinner by thee remembered.
Thou hast led us out of darkness into light.
Lord! My sin and my guilt,
Take them and remove them.
O God, O God, O God, Amen!

SEVEN CLASSES OF YEZIDIS

They are divided into seven classes, and each class has functions peculiar to itself that cannot be discharged by any of the other classes. They are:

1. Šeiḫ. He is the servant of the tomb, and a descendant of Imam Ḥasan al-Baṣrî. No one can give a legal decision or sign any document except the šeiḫ who is the servant of Šeiḫ 'Adî's tomb. He has a sign by which he is distinguished from others. The sign is a belt which he puts on his body, and net-like gloves, which resemble the halters of camels. If he goes among his people, they bow down and pay him their respects. The šeiḫs sell a place in paradise to anyone who wishes to pay money.

2. Emir. The emirship specifically belongs to the descendants of Yezîd. They have a genealogical tree, preserved from their fathers and forefathers, which goes up to Yezîd himself. The emirs have charge of the temporal and governmental affairs, and have the right to say, "Do this and do not that."

3. Ḳawwâl. He has charge of tambourines and flutes and religious hymns.

4. Pîr. To him appertain the conduct of fasts, the breaking of fasts, and hair-dressing.

5. Kôchak. To him appertain the duties of religious

instruction, and sepulture, and interpretation of dreams, i. e., prophecy.

6. Faḳîr. To him appertain the duties of instruction of boys and girls in playing on the tambourines, in dancing and religious pleasure. He serves Šeiḫ 'Adî.

7. Mulla. To him appertain the duties of instructing children. He guards the books and the mysteries of religion and attends to the affairs of the sect.

ARTICLES OF FAITH

At one time (A. H. 1289; A. D. 1872), the Ottoman power wanted to draft from among them an army instead of taking the tax which was its due. They presented to the government all the rules that prevented them from complying. These all pertain to religion and are moral obligations upon them. They are as follows:

Article I

According to our Yezidi religion every member of our sect, whether big or little, girl or woman, must visit Melek Ṭâ'ûs three times a year, that is, first, from the beginning to the last of the month of April, Roman calendar; secondly, from the beginning to the end of the month of September; thirdly, from the beginning to the end of the month of November. If anyone visit not the image of Melek Ṭâ'ûs, he is an infidel.

Article II

If any member of our sect, big or little, visit not his highness Šeih 'Adî bn Musâfir—may God sanctify his mysteries! once a year, i. e., from the fifteenth to the twentieth of the month of September, Roman calendar, he is an infidel according to our religion.

Article III

Every member of our sect must visit the place of the sunrise every day when it appears, and there should not be Moslem, nor Christian, nor any one else in that place. If any one do this not, he is an infidel.

Article IV

Every member of our sect must daily kiss the hand of his brother, his brother of the next world, namely, the servant of the Mahdi, and the hand of his šeiḥ or *pîr*. If any one do this not, he is regarded as an infidel.

Article V

According to our religion it is something intolerable when the Moslem in the morning begins to say in prayer, God forbid! "I take refuge in God, etc."[38] If any one of us hear it, he must kill the one who says it and kill himself; otherwise he becomes an infidel.

Article VI

When one of our sect is on the point of death, if there be no brother of the next world and his šeiḥ, or his *pîr* and one of the *ḳawwâls* with him to say three sayings over him, viz.; "O servant of Melek Ṭâ'ûs, whose ways are high, you must die in the religion of the one we worship, who is Melek Ṭâ'ûs, whose ways are high, and do not die in any other religion than his. And if some one should come and say to you something from the Mohammedan religion, or Christian religion, or Jewish religion, or some other religion, do not believe him, and do not follow him. And if you believe and follow another religion than that of the one we worship, Melek Ṭâ'ûs, you shall die an infidel," he becomes an infidel.

Article VII

We have something called the blessing of Šeih 'Adî, that is, the dust of the tomb Šeih 'Adî—may God sanctify his mystery! Every member of our sect must have some of it with him in his pocket and eat of it every morning. And if he eat not of it intentionally, he is an infidel. Likewise at the time of death, if he possess not some of that dust intentionally, he dies an infidel.

Article VIII

Regarding our fasting, if any one of our sect wish to fast, he must fast in his own place, not in another. For while fasting he must go every morning to the house of his šeih and his *pîr*, and there he must begin to fast; and when he breaks his fast, likewise, he must go to the house of his šeih and his *pîr*, and there break the fast by drinking the holy wine of the šeih or the *pîr*. And if he drink not two or three glasses of that wine, his fasting is not acceptable, and he becomes an infidel.

Article IX

If one of our sect go to another place and remain there as much as one year, and afterward return to his place, then his wife is forbidden him, and none of us will give him a wife. If anyone give him a wife, that one is an infidel.

Article X

Regarding our dress, as we have mentioned in the fourth Article that every one of our sect has a brother for the next world, he has also a sister for the next world.[59] Therefore if any one of us make for himself a new shirt, it is necessary that his sister for the next world should open its neck band, i. e., the neck band of that shirt, with her hand. And if she open it not with her hand, and he wear it, then he is an infidel.

Article XI

If some one of our sect make a shirt or a new dress, he cannot wear it without baptizing it in the blessed water which is to be found at the shrine of his highness Šeih 'Adî may God sanctify his mystery! If he wear it, he is an infidel.

Article XII

We may not wear a light black dress at all. We may not comb our heads with the comb of a Moslem or a Christian or a Jew or any other. Nor may we shave our heads with the razor used by any other than ourselves (Yezidis), except it be washed in the blessed water which is to be found at the shrine of his highness Šeih 'Adî. Then it is lawful for us to shave our heads. But if we shave our heads without the razor having been washed in that water, we become infidels.

Article XIII

No Yezidi may enter the water-closet of a Moslem, or take a bath at a Moslem's house, or eat with a Moslem spoon or drink from a Moslem's cup, from a cup used by any one of another sect. If he does, he is an infidel.[40]

Article XIV

Concerning food, there is a great difference between us and the other sects. We do not eat meat or fish, squash, *bamia* (okra), *fasulia* (beans), cabbage, or lettuce. We cannot even dwell in the place where lettuce is sown.[41]

For these and other reasons, we cannot enter the military service, etc.

The names of those who affixed their signatures:

THE HEAD OF THE YEZIDI SECT, THE EMIR OF ŠEIḪÂN, ḤUSEIN.

THE RELIGIOUS ŠEIḪ OF THE YEZIDI SECT OF THE DISTRICT OF ŠEIḪÂN, ŠEIḪ NAṢIR.

THE CHIEF OF THE VILLAGE OF MAM REŠÂN, PÎR SULEIMÂN.

THE VILLAGE CHIEF OF MUSKÂN, MURAD.
" " " " ḤATÂRAH, AYYÛB.
" " " " BEIBÂN, ḤUSEIN.
" " " " DAHḲAN, ḤASSAN.
" " " " ḤUZRÂN, NU'MÔ.
" " " " BÂKASRA, 'ALI.
" " " " BÂ'AŠÎḲA, JAMÔ.
" " " " ḤÔŠÂBA, ILIAS.
" " " " KREPAḤIN, SAĜD.
" " " " ḲABÂREH, KÔCHAK.
" " " " ḲASÔ.
" " " " SINÂ, 'ABDÔ.
" " " " 'AIN SIFNI, GURGÔ.
" " " " ḲASR-'IZZ-AD-DÎN.
" " " " ḤEIRÔ.
" " " " KIBERTÔ, ṬÂHIR.

AND OTHERS.

These are they whose names were in the petition above mentioned, and from which we copied a few things

The result was that when they presented this petition, they were exempted from military service, but they paid a tax in money as did the Christians.

NOTES ON PART I

[1] A. H. 295 (A. D. 807–8). This is the date of Al-Muktadir's accession, who reigned till A. H. 320 (A. D. 932); cf. W. Muir, *The Caliphate*, p. 559.

[2] The life of Manṣûr-al-Ḥallâj is given in Fihrist (ed. Flügel), p. 190.

[3] The life of 'Abd-al-Kâdir of Jîlân is given in Jami's *Nafahat* (ed. Lee), p. 584.

[4] The Hakkari country is a dependency of Mosul, and inhabited by Kurds and Nestorians; cf. p. 104. Ibn Ḥaukal, Kîtâb al-Masâlik wal-Mamâlik (ed. M. J. De Goeje), pp. 143 f.

[5] Yakût, IV, 373, calls it Laileš and says that Šeiḫ 'Adî lived there.

[6] Presumably Yezîd bn Mu'âwiya, the second caliph in the Omayyid dynasty, who reigned, A. D. 680-83; cf. W. Muir, *The Caliphate*, p. 327.

[7] The life of Ḥasan al-Baṣrî is given in Ibn Hallikân. He is not to be identified with Ḥasan al-Baṣrî (died 110 A. H., who, according to Mohammedan tradition, first pointed the Koran text, with the assistance of Yaḥyâ bn Yamar.

[8] In Menant's *Yzidis*, 48, the names of these seven angels are somewhat differently given. According to Mohammedan tradition Zazil or Azazil was the original name of the devil.

[9] By the "throne" here is meant the throne of God, and by the "carpet" the earth; cf. Sura 60: 131.

[10] According to Moslem belief, wheat was the forbidden fruit; see Baiḍâwi on Sura, ii, 33.

[11] Kunsiniyat is an obscure term.

[12] 'Ain Sifni is about five miles from Ba'adrie; cf. Layard, *Nineveh*, I, 272.

[13] Yaḳût (III, 158) mentions a similar tradition.

[14] These are indications of Mohammedan influence and censorship, for no Yezidi will ever write in his sacred book such words as Šeitân, Šar, etc.

[15] That is, those of other religions.

[16] Sanjaḳ is a Turkish word, meaning banner; it is the name by which the Yezidis generally designate the sacred image of Melek Ṭâ'ûs.

[17] See note 27.

[18] The Harranian New Year fell on the first day of April, and on the sixth day they slaughtered an ox and ate it; cf. Fihrist, 322.

[19] A similar practice is found among the Parsees of India, who hang a string of leaves across the entrances to their houses at the beginning of every New Year.

[20] According to Babylonian mythology, human destiny was decreed on the New Year's day and sealed on the tenth day; cf. the *Hibbert Journal*, V, January, 1907. And according to Talmud (Mišna, Roš hašana, 1:2), New Year's is the most important judgment day, on which all creatures pass for judgment before the Creator. On this day three books are opened, wherein the fate of the wicked, the righteous, and those of the intermediate class are recorded. Hence prayer and works of repentance are performed at the New Year from the first to the tenth days, that an unfavorable decision might be averted; cf. *Jewish Encyclopedia*, 'Penitential Day." R. Akiba says: "On New Year day all men are judged; and the decree is sealed on the Day of Atonement;" cf. *ibid.*, "Day of Joudgment."

[21] Ibrîḳ al-Asfar means "the yellow pitcher."

[22] Bakbûḳ is a pitcher with a narrow spout.

[23] Mar Mattie is a Syrian monastery about seven hours' ride east of Mosul, generally known by the name of Šeiḫ Mattie, in accordance with the general custom of sheltering a Christian saint beneath a Moslem title. Elijah is known as Al-Ḫuder, "the green one." Aphrates was bishop of Šeiḫ Mattie. The church of this monastery is a large building, chiefly interesting as containing the tomb of the great Bar Hebraeus, known as Abu-l-Faraj, who was ordained at Tripolis, and became in 1246 A. D. Metropolitan of Mosul. He lies buried, with his brother Barsom, in the "Beth Kadišeh (sanctuary) of the church, and over them is placed the inscription: "This is the grave of Mar Gregorias, and of Mar Barsome his brother, the children of the Hebrew, on Mount Elpep" (the Syriac name for Jabal Maḳlûb).

[24] *Kani* in Kurdish means a spring; *zarr*, yellow. In Kurdish, as in Persian, the adjective usually follows the modified noun; cf. Tartibi Jadid, Ta'alimi Faresi. *The New Method for Teaching Persian* (in the Turkish language, ed. Kasbar, Constantinople, A. H. 1312), p. 18.

[25] Jawîš is a Turkish word, signifying a sergeant.

[26] This ceremony, as well as the names 'Arafat, Zamzam, etc., seems to be a mere copy of the Meccah Pilgrimage. 'Arafât, "The Mount of Recognition," is situated twelve miles from Mecca, a place where the pilgrims stay on the ninth day of the day of the pilgrimage, and recite the midday and afternoon prayer. The Mohammedan legend says, that when our first parents forfeited heaven for eating wheat, they were cast down from the Paradise, Adam fell on the Isle of Ceylon, and Eve near Jiddah (the port of Mecca) in Arabia; and that, after separation of 200 years, Adam was conducted by the Angel Gabriel to a mountain near Mecca, where he found and knew

his wife, the mountain being then named 'Arafat, "Recognition."

[27] The god Nisroch of Scripture, II Kings 19:37; Isa. 37: 38.

[29] A superstitious name signifying an ill omen.

[30] That is, public prayers like those of the Mohammedans and of the Christians; cf. Al Mašrik, II, 313.

[31] The text has "her hand."

[32] While the Yezidis venerate 'Abd al-Kâdir of Jîlân, the Nusairis curse him; cf. *JAOS*, VIII, 274.

[33] This belief is taken from Mohammedanism.

[34] The Arabs worshiped a deity under the form of a *nasr* (eagle), Aš-Šahrastânî, II, 434; Yaḳut, IV, 780; *The Syriac Doctrine of Addai* (ed. George Philips), p. 24.

[35] Cf. Gen. 1: 2, and the Babylonian Creation Epic.

[36] That is the spring of Šeiḫ 'Adî.

[37] The reference is to Jabal Maḳlûb, which, according to the Yezidi belief, moved from its place near Lališ to enable every Yezidi, wherever he may be, to direct his morning prayers toward the tomb of 'Adî.

[38] The Moslem begins his prayer by cursing the devil.

[39] That is a person of the same faith, a Yezidi.

[40] A Nusairi, on the contrary, may become a Mohammedan with a Mohammedan, a Christian with a Christian, and a Jew with a Jew; cf. *JAOS*, VII, 298.

[41] The Sabians did not eat purslane, garlic, beans, cauliflower, cabbage, and lentis; cf. Bar. Hebraeus, At-Târîḫ, ed. A. Ṣalḥani, Beirut, 1890, 266.

PART II

THE CRITICAL DISCUSSION OF YEZIDISM

THIS PAGE LEFT BLANK BY ORIGINAL PUBLISHER, USE FOR NOTES

CHAPTER I

The Religious Origin of the Yezidis

The origin of the devil-worshippers has been the subject of much controversy; but aside from an expression of views, no satisfactory solution of the problem has as yet been reached. The different theories which have been advanced may be classified under four general heads: The Myth of the Yezidis themselves; the tradition of Eastern Christians; the dogmatic idea of the Mohammedan scholars; and the speculative theory of the western orientalists.

I

The Yezidi Myth

The Myth of the Yezidis concerning their origin may be derived from three different sources: from their sacred book, from the appendix of the manuscript, and from actual conversation of travellers with them or with natives dweling among them. One noticeable fact is that this tradition assumes the religion of the sect as existing long before the time of their chief saint, Šeiḫ 'Adî. Al-Jilwah begins with the statement that Melek Ṭâ'ûs sent his servant, *i. e.*, the Yezidis, that they might not go astray. Starting from this assumption, the writer of the revealed book goes on to trace the origin of the "elect" to the very beginning of human history. He asserts that from the start God created them as a peculiar people of 'Azazil, *i. e.*, Melek-Ṭâ'ûs. In the main, this idea finds expression in the oral traditions. But here we have a mass of material so clouded by superstition and ignorance that it is next to impossible to come to any conclusion as to the history of this interesting people. One point the myth repeatedly emphasizes, as an explanation of the origin of the sect, is that it was descended from Adam alone; while the other sects were descended from Adam and Eve. For this reason, the same tradition implies, the Yezidis are nobler than the others. But how they have come to be such unique descendants is a question not easily answered. One account has it that when Adam and Eve disputed as to the generation of the human race, each claiming to be the sole begetter of the race, they finally agreed to put their seed in separate jars and seal them with their own seals. After nine months they opened the jars, and in Adam's jar they found two children, a male and a female. From these two the Yezidis were descended. Another explanation is that from Adam's essence was born Šeher bn Jebr, of whom nothing is known; and of him, a separate community, which is the sect of Melek Ṭâ'ûs. We have, moreover, the tradition that the Yezidis are descendants of a son born to Adam of his spittle. Now whether this son be identical with Šeher bn Jebr is not certain. Writing in one of the oriental periodicals, an eastern scholar quotes a Yezidi šeiḫ in a statement which seems to corroborate the tradition that the Yezidis are a noble progeny of Adam; but the quotation differs from the instance previously cited in stating that the quarrel which took place between Adam and Eve led to their separation to places distant from each other a journey of forty days.[1] There, it is said, Adam miraculously gave birth to a son. Distressed by this incident, Eve asked God that she might find favor in her husband's eyes by giving birth to a child. Thereupon, it continues, she begot a very pretty daughter. Attracted by her beauty, Adam married her to his son. Now, the Yezidis, we are told, are the blessed seed of these two children.[2]

Not only when the tradition, tracing the origin of the Yezidis as a race, asserts that, as a religious body, they come from a very ancient time; but also when it speaks of them as a nation, it points out their antiquity. On this latter, as well as on the former point, their book and their oral tradition agree. The Yezidis are said to have sprung from a noble personage, the King of Peace, whose name was Na-'umi, but whom they now call Melek-Miran.[3] The rest of mankind, however, are from the seed of Ham, who mocked his father. Whom they signified by Na-'umi or Miran it is hard to say; but it is likely that they regard him as one of the other two sons of Noah. They claim also that the ancient Assyrian kings were members of their race, and that some of the Persian, Roman and Jewish kings were appointed for them by Melek Ṭâ'ûs. They likewise seem to trace their origin to the prophets and other personages of the Old Testament; as Seth, Enoch, Noah, etc. Their religion furthermore, they assert, antedates Christ.[4]

There is still another tradition that traces the devil-worshippers to a different origin. I refer to the statement which Maṣehaf Reš makes regarding Mu'awiya, Mohammed's servant.[5] Mu'awiya was asked by his master to shave his head. While performing the duty, he cut the prophet's scalp, and began to lick the bleeding spot. When he was told that this act would result in his giving birth to a nation which would oppose the followers of his master, Mu'Awiya declared that he would not marry. He was afterwards, however, bitten by a serpent, and was told that he would die unless he married. He therefore consented to marry, but chose an old woman in order not to have children. But she miraculously became a young woman of twenty-five. And from her the God Yezid was born. The story, of course, is a myth, and it is of such a nature that no historic fact can be derived from it. It is further complicated by the fact that this Yezid is indentified with Melek Ṭâ'ûs; and, in another myth, is represented in form as being half angel and half man and as remaining a bachelor long after the marriage of Adam. He was, however, finally possessed of a desire to marry, and, unable to marry a mortal's daughter, being himself half angel, sought the assistance of Melek Ṭâ'ûs, who presented to him an ḥouri, and from this union there sprang a pious people, the Yezidis.

But the devil-worshippers have still another story, which goes to show that Yezid bn Mu'awiya is not their founder. This myth asserts that they are the progeny of Adam's son who was married to Eve's daughter; that the descendants continued worshipping God and Melek Ṭâ'ûs without bringing a foreign element into their religion; and that, at first, the sect did not bear the name Yezidis, which, in their own opinion, is a comparatively new appellative. As to how they came to be called by this new name, it is explained that when, in the course of time, some corruption entered the Yezidi religion, there arose a certain Calif by the name of Yezid who wrought miracles. Since then, his followers have been called Yezidis. This Yezid, it is said, is the son of Mu'awiya bn Sufian, and his mother was of Christian origin. To accomplish his desire, bn Mu'awiya went to Šeiḫ 'Adi, who was a learned and devout but cunning person, and had instituted a religious innovation. Yezid, the tradition continues, learned 'Adi's religion and taught it to his followers; and, from that time on, the sect came to be called after him.[6] But while some, considering this legend as authoritative, venerate the man bearing the name, others deny all connection with him.[7]

The testimony of some travellers offers another explanation of the origin of the sect in question, an account which has perhaps more historical significance than the preceding theories. It is stated that the Yezidis have a tradition to the effect that they came from Baṣrah and from the country watered by the lower part of the Euphrates; that after their emigration they first settled in Syria, and subsequently took possession of the Sinjar Hill and the district now inhabited in Kurdistan. As to the date of their settlement in Mesopotamia, no positive information can be obtained. Some scholars infer that it took place about the time of Tamerlane, toward the end of the fourteenth century.[8] It is related that the devil-worshippers hold that, among their own number, the ancient name for God is Azd, and from it the name of the sect is derived;[9] that the conviction that they are Yezidis, *i. e.*, God's people, has been their consolation and comfort through the ages in their tribulations;[10] and that they have taken many religious observances from different bodies—Mohammedans, Christians, Jews, Pagan Arabs, Shiites, and Sabaians.

Besides these different explanations of the origin of the devil-worshippers as descendants of Adam, of Yezid bn Mu'awiya, as being of the colony from the north, as taking their name from Azd, God, there is another account. I refer to a myth which is current among the people of Seistan, an eastern province of

Persia, where there are a considerable number of these Shaitan parasts (devil worshippers):

"In former times there existed a prophet named Ḥanalalah, whose life was prolonged to the measure of a thousand years. He was their ruler and benefactor; and as by his agency, their flocks gave birth to lambs and kids miraculously once a week, though ignorant of the use of money, they, with much gratitude to him, procured all the comforts of life. At length, however, he died, and was succeeded by his son, whom Šatan, presuming on his inexperience, tempted to sin by entering a large mulberry tree, when he addressed the successor of Ḥanalalah, and called on him to worship the prince of darkness. Astonished, yet unshaken, the youth resisted the temptation. But the miracle proved too much for the constancy of his flock, who now began to turn to the worship of the devil. The young prophet, enraged at this, seized an axe and a saw, and prepared to cut down the tree. He was arrested in this by the appearance of a human being, who exclaimed, 'Rash boy, desist! Turn to me and let us wrestle for the victory. If you conquer, then fell the tree.'

"The prophet contended and vanquished his opponent, who, however, bought his own safety and that of the tree by the promise of a large weekly treasure. After seven days the holy victor again visited the tree to claim the gold or fell it to the ground; but Satan persuaded him to hazard another struggle on the promise that, if he conquered again, the amount should be doubled. This second encounter proved fatal to the youth. He was put to death by his spiritual antagonist, and the result confirmed the tribes over whom he had ruled in their worship of the tree and its tutelary demon."[11]

According to this legend, the Šatan parasts are the victims of their young prophet who, as long as he was actuated by a disinterested zeal for religion, was victorious over the principle of evil; but failed as soon as that zeal gave place to a sordid cupidity for earthly treasure.

I have dwelt upon the superstitious theories of the Yezidis themselves regarding their religious origin, not because these theories have an importance in themselves, but because of their bearing upon the views advanced by modern scholars. The scholars have based their theories on some of these conflicting stories without sufficient criticism. I shall dwell upon this more at length later on.

II

The Christian Tradition

But the myth of the Yezidis is not the only account that attempts to trace their religious origin; the eastern Christians have a tradition that gives a different interpretation. It is to the effect that the people in question were originally Christians, but that ignorance brought them into their present condition. The tradition runs that the shrine of Šeiḫ 'Adi was formerly a Nestorian monastery which was noted for the devotion of its monks, but that these were tempted by the devil and left their convent. The Church of the Monastery was dedicated to St. Thaddeus or Addai,[22] one of the seventy-two disciples who, after the ascension of our Lord, was sent to King Abgar of Edessa. It is said that the temple of 'Adi has a conventicle resembling that at Jerusalem.[13] The story of how the cloister was deserted is as follows:

On a great feast day, while the hermits bearing the cross went in procession around the church, they saw, hanging on a tree, a piece of paper with this inscription: "O ye devout monks! Let it be known to you that God has forgiven all your sins, great and small; cease to undergo religious exercises; leave your hermitage; disperse, marry and rear children. Peace be unto you!" On the second day they observed the same thing, and were led to dispute among themselves whether this were a device of God or of a devil. When on the third day the same incident was repeated, they agreed to leave the abbey and follow what seemed to them a divine order. Šeiḫ 'Adi, the legend goes on, had foretold to the Yezidis of that district that the monks of this monastery would desert their place, would become Yezidis, would marry and beget children; that he would die during that time; and that he wishes his followers to pull down the altar of the church in that priory and bury him there. Shortly after the fulfilment of his prophecy, the Šeiḫ died, and was entombed in the place of the altar. And since that time, it is asserted, the spot has become the sanctuary of the devil-worshippers. In support of this statement, it is argued, that there was a Syriac inscription in the temple mentioning the name of the founder of the monastery and the patriarch in whose time it was built; that some of the Yezids themselves bear testimony to this fact, and say they have removed the writing from its former place and have hidden it at the entrance to 'Adi's temple, a spot the whereabouts of which only a few of them know. The reason why this record is hidden, it is explained, is the fear that the Nestorians may see it and reclaim the church.[14]

Such is the eastern Christian's tradition relative to the origin of the Yezidis. It is, of course, merely a legend; but its character is such as to require careful examination and critical study. It may embody a measure of truth that will indirectly throw some light on the subject in hand.

One noticeable thing regarding this current view is that it is not a recent invention; else it might be said to be the creation of ignorance at a time far removed from the event which it records. Assemani, himself an oriental of distinguished scholarship, in that part of his book wherein he treats of the religion of Mesopotamia, according to the natives of the country, says that the Yezidis were at one time Christians, who, however, in the course of time, had forgotten the fundamental principles of their faith.[15] This statement is incorporated in the writings of all western orientals that have travelled in the East.[16]

Another thing worthy of notice is that the Christians should have such a sacred regard for his tradition as to hand it down to posterity at the risk of their own reputation. Certainly the Christians are not cherishing this theory with any expectation of receiving honor by assuming relation with the Yezidis. The devil-worshippers are utterly despised by all their neighbors. Nor do they do it out of love, that they may arouse the sympathy of the dominating race for this degraded people. Oriental Christians themselves despise the Yezidi sect. They would not, and could not, help them. There must then be some truth in a legend that leads the church to regard a despised people as having been at one time co-religionists.

Were the antiquity of the tradition, and the unfavorable result which its entertainment causes, the only two reasons for its consideration, we might just as well dismiss it. But there are other things which go to point out some historic facts underlying the current theory. One such fact is that the family name of the Yezidis around Mosul is Daseni, plur Dawasen. The Christians and the Mohammedans know them by this name, and they themselves also use it, and say it is the ancient name of their race, existing from time immemorial.[17] Now Daseni, or Dasaniyat, was the name of a Nestorian Diocese, the disappearance of which is simultaneous with the appearance of the Yezidis in these places.[18]

It is stated, moreover, that all the people of Sinjar were formerly Christians, belonging to the ancient Syriac Church and having a very prominent diocese, which was called the diocese of Šaki, *i. e.*, Sinjar; and that the diocese continued to exist till the middle of the eighteenth century: What goes to verify this tradition is that, at present, there is a library at Jabal Sinjar, under the control of the Yezidis, that consists of ancient Syriac books. They are kept in a small room guarded by a Yezidi. On Sunday and Friday of every week they burn incense and light lamps in honor of the manuscripts; and once a month they take them out in the sun to dust and to preserve them from destruction by dampness. After the door is locked, the key is kept by the Šeiḫ, besides whom and his son no one else is allowed to touch the books. What is more interesting, the people of Sinjar say they have inherited the library from their forefathers, who were Christians.[19] It is pointed out, furthermore, that the names of the principal towns of the Yezidis are Syriac. Ba'šika comes from "the house of the falsely accused, or oppressed"; Ba'adrie from "the place of help or refuge"; Baḥzanie from "the house of visions or inspiration"; Talḥas from "the hill of suffering," where many Christians were martyred by Persians. These are a few of many Yezidi villages having Syriac names.

The Yezidis have religious practices which are to be found only in the Christian Church. I mean the rites of baptism and the Eucharist. It is true that the use of water as a rite is practised by other non-Christian sects, such as the Mandeans; but it is argued that this ordinance as observed by the Yezidis is so similar to that of the Christians that its origin is to be traced back to Christianity, rather than to any other system. Like their neighbors, the Dawaseni must if possible baptize their children at the earliest age. In performing the rite, the Šeiḫ, like the Christian priest, puts his hand upon the child's head. In regard to the sacrament of the Lord's supper, it is strictly Christian in character. The Yezidis call the cup the cup of Isa (Jesus); and when a couple marry, they go to a Christian town to partake of Al-Ḳiddas (the Eucharist) from the hand of a priest, a custom which prevails among eastern Christians. What requires special note is that this practice is observed where the Yezidi influence is not very strong, a fact which seems to indicate that the Apostate Nasara, who lived remote from strongly Yezidising influences, were able to retain some of their originally much favored practices, and vice versa.[20]

Finally, the Dawaseni entertain great reverence for Christianity and the Christian saints. They respect the churches and tombs of the Christians, and kiss the doors and walls when they enter them; but they never visit a Mohammedan mosque. In the Black Book a statement is made that on her way to the house of her bridegroom, a bride should visit the temple of every idol she passes by, even if it be a Christian Church.[21] They have also professed reverence for

'Isa (Jesus). They affect more attachment to An-Naṣara than to Mohammedans. Such a religious affinity cannot be fully accounted for on any other ground than that of their sincere respect for Christainity, a feeling which clearly indicates that these people must at one time have had a very close connection with Christianity. This intimate relation cannot be explained by their ignorance, or by kindred experiences, as some scholars seem to think.[22] It is true the Christians have been co-sufferers with them; both have lived for generations under the same yoke of bondage and oppression and under similar circumstances. But this alone could not create sympathy between them. Such an assumption cannot be verified by the facts collected through our observation of the Yezidis' character as a religious body. They are sincere in their beliefs, and never compromise in religious matters. History has shown again and again that they have suffered martyrdom for their faith, in which they have been as sincere and unshaken as have been the heroes of any religion. No matter how uneducated they may be, they are not hypocrites in their faith. The theory is also refuted by our understanding of the nature of the affinity in question between the Yezidis and the Christians. It is not a matter of sympathy but of religion. They believe in some forms of Christianity; and when they visit a church, they want to exercise their faith and not to express their sympathy. What is more, the eastern Christians have no sympathy for the devil worshippers, at least, not more than they have for any other religious body. Such an affinity is wanting between the Jews and the Christians or the Yezidis, yet they all live under the same conditions.

I am not here advocating the theory, or implying, that the Yezidi sect is a corrupt form of Christianity, but am simply aiming to show that if the similarity of a certain religion with another in some phases be taken as a ground for the explanation of its origin, the Christian tradition can be regarded as a more probable theory to account for the rise of Yezidism than any other view: And, hence, to point out, what seems to me to be the best position, that the explanation must be found ultimately in some historical document which will give us a reasonable clew in the tracing of the sect in question to its founder.

III

The Speculative Theories of Western Orientalists

Thus far we have been dealing with the different theories regarding the origin of the Yezidis held in the East: the myth of the devil-worshippers themselves, the Christian tradition. Now we turn our attention to the West, which also has expressed itself on this subject. The degree of interest shown in this particular case, however, differs with different nationalities. The English-speaking scholars come first; next come the French; then the Russians; and finally the Italians. The German scholars seem to be interested mainly in certain words and festive events. And, in the discussion of these, they go so far in their unbounded speculation that one cannot tell whether the people they deal with are the Yezidis in question, Assyrians, Babylonians, Canaanites, Greeks, Romans or Jews. The German writers do not seem to be interested so much in the problem of the origin of this people as a sect, unless they regard the question as settled on the ground of the Yezidis' own statement that they are the descendants of Yezid bn Mu'awiya.

To tell the truth, the rise of the interest in the inquiry about the founder of this sect on a scientific basis, is due, without question, to the scholarship of the West. And any solution of the problem (and it does not matter who does the work), in the last analysis, must be accredited to the influences emanating from these scholars and these scholars only. Nevertheless modern orientalists have been far from approaching the solution of the question. This may be due in part to the extreme interest which they have taken in the matter, an interest which led them to accept the phenomena without critical examination. But the inductive study of their respective writings tends to show that this is due to their method of procedure rather than to anything else. They have employed the philosophical and not the historical method.[23] I do not mean to deny the value of such a course of investigation in questions pertaining to religion, but what I do mean to say is that the method of the scholars in question is almost purely speculative, and they do not seem to appeal to historical facts in support of their assumptions. The inevitable consequence has been, therefore, that in their theories there exists an uncertainty and indefiniteness that puzzles the student of history.

Another fact which the inductive study of the views of the western scholars reveals is that their theories are nothing more nor less than the expression of the Yezidis' tradition in terms of modern scholarship, without, however, the showing of reasons for so doing. This fact will be proved presently when we shall examine their respective writings.

Western orientalists are divided into three schools of opinion on the question of the religious origin of the Yezidis. There are those who hold that the sect takes its rise from Yezid bn Mu'awiya. This view is advocated by a modern writer, who says, "The Arabs who accepted Mohammed called those who did not Al-jahaleen, *i. e.,* the ignorant ones. Among the latter was Yezid bn Mu'awiya who refused to accompany Mu'awiya, his father, as an attendant upon his person. Many of the ignorant ones rallied around Yezid, and he became the nucleus of the sect that appropriated his name. The Yezidis possess a genealogical tree by means of which they trace their religious origin back to him."[84]

Now, the ground for this assertion, the writer does not give; he is entirely silent as to the source of his information. It is evident, therefore, that he is regarding the superstitious theory of the Yezidis as a fact without making any reflection upon it. He also seems to be confusing this Yezid with his uncle of the same name, who, with Mu'awiya his brother came in company with their father Abu Sofian, to Mohammed to receive presents from the Prophet. But the Arab historians tell us that not only Abu Sofian and each of his two sons received a hundred camels but that they were each presented with forty ounces of silver.[25]

Then, too, many scholars deny that the name Yezidis is the original appellation. Some assert it was put upon them by the Mohammedans as a term of reproach.[26] Others maintain that the sect adopted the name Yezid, son of Mu'awiya to secure toleration at the hands of the Mohammedans.[27] But the scholar quoted may entertain the view of those who say that the Yezidis are really the followers of Ibn Mu'awiya; but that they deny it for fear of persecution on the part of Shiites. These latter hate Yezid, because he murdered 'Ali's son, Husein, who is regarded by them as their true Imam. This inference is founded on the theory that the Mohammedans of Persia consider the people in question as descendants of the Calif whose name is odious to them.[28] But it is not certain that the followers of 'Ali entertain such a view regarding the origin of the Yezidis. And, if they do, they have no historical facts to justify them in their opinion. Their hatred of the sect can be better explained on the basis of the relation of the devil-worshippers to Yezid bn Unaisa. For he was one of those who most bitterly hated 'Ali; see pp. 121, 122, 128 of this book.

Furthermore, the theory of this school is neutralized by the fact that none of the Arab historians mentions the son of the first Calif in the Omayyid dynasty as a founder of any heretical sect. On the contrary, they all agree that he was not only a Mohammedan but a successor of the prophet, being the second calif in the Omayyid dynasty. Ibn Ḫallikan mentions his name two or three times, and says that his works were collected. He says nothing, however, as to his founding any religious schism.

There is still another school among the western orientalists. I mean those who hold that the religion of the devil-worshippers is of Persian origin. They are of two wings. There are those who take their method of procedure from the name Yezid or Yazd. They argue that this term in Persian, Yazd (pla Yazdân), Avestan Yezata, 'worthy of worship', means God, or good spirit, over against Ahriman, the evil principle. Hence, the name Yezid, according to them, indicates the people that believe in this good god. To the objection that the Yezidis worship the evil spirit, answer is made that Yezid Ferfer is the name of the attendant of the evil spirit among the Parsees.[29] Others believe that the word "Yezid" signifies God. It indicates in the plural the observers of superstitious doctrines as may be seen by the idol Yezid, which the Bishop of Nagham overthrew.[30] Still others say that in the tradition of these people Yezid must have been an abbreviated form of Aez-da-Khuda, that is, created of God. In support of this theory, it is claimed that in reality the Yezidis worship God and not the devil. It is thought by many, too, that the Yezidis derive their name from Yazd, or Yezid, a name of a town in Central Persia, of which the Parsees form the principal part of the inhabitants.[31]

The other wing of the second school attempts to trace the origin of the devil-worshippers to a Persian source on the basis of certain resemblances between the two religions. Conspicuous among the representatives of this school is Professor A. V. Jackson, of Columbia University. This distinguished scholar is considered an eminent authority on Iranian religions, and particularly an eye-witness authority on the Yezidi question. His views, therefore, not only deserve careful consideration, but they demand their full share in solving such an important problem as the one under discussion. I have preferred his discussion of this theory to that of others because he has expressed himself clearly and consistently and without rendering himself liable to misapprehension on the part of the reader. Briefly stated, Dr. Jackson's position is as follows: "The Yezidis may actually show some surviving traces of old devil-worship in Mazandaran, which Zoroaster anathematized so bitterly," and "some old reminiscences of common Iranian faith." To verify this hypothesis, he proceeds to point out many instances. One example he cites is that "the Yezidis are shocked if one spits upon the earth, because they interpret this as an insult to the devil." He traces this abhorrence to "Zoroastrian prescription, forbidding the earth in any way to be defiled." "The Daevayasna or devil-worshippers in Avesta," he goes on to say, "may indirectly have had a kindred notion, *i. e.*, not mentioning the name of Satan." Moreover this American critic is informed that the Yezidis "believe in a father primeval, that lived before Adam, and did not fall into sin." And this information leads him to think that such a notion helps "the Zoroastrian student to recognize at once a far-off reminiscence of Avestan Gaya-Mashai, the Iranian Adam and Eve."[31]

One noticeable thing in favor of the two schools is that their method is strictly scientific, in the modern sense of the term. It is a posteriori and not a priori; it is inductive. Yet however scientific their method may seem to be their conclusions cannot be accepted as final. For the inductive method, according to the great French scientist, Poincaré, cannot give us exact knowledge because its experiments do not cover all the instances in a given case. There can be only a partial verification. There will always remain some phenomena that cannot be brought within the sphere of a particular observation.[32] Now, this is exactly the case in the subject under consideration. Only in some phases does the Yezidi religion resemble that of the old Persians. There are other beliefs which do not come under this category, and which seem to bear the traces of some other religions. What are we to do with these?[33] The advocates of the theory in question admit that such is the case, but they assert that "the resemblances of the Yezidi religion to Christianity and Islam are accidental"; that "owing to the residence of the Yezidis among the Mohammedans, the sect naturally has much in common with Islam."[34] But why are the resemblances to Iranism not to be accounted for in the same way as those to other religions? Why may not equally strong inference be made from the likeness to Christianity? And what is the basis of such a discrimination? On these questions we are left entirely in the dark. Now, it is this lack of ground for their method of procedure that leads one to seek the solution of the problem on some other verifiable hypothesis.

There is still another school among the western orientalists. I refer to those who maintain that the Yezidi sect was founded by Šeiḫ 'Adi. A modern writer who holds this theory, after critically reviewing the views held by the different scholars, proceeds to advance his own idea. To emhasize it, and leave no room for further criticism, he claims that the theory has been "generally" accepted. To quote:

"It is generally agreed upon that the sect of the Yezidis was founded by Šeiḫ 'Adi. He is a historical personage, but it is exceedingly difficult, and almost impossible, to establish any historical facts out of the mist of very fantastic stories current about him."[35]

He supports his notion by an appeal to an Arab

author, Kasi Ahmad ibn-Ḫallikan, from whom, according to this writer, an extract relating to Šeiḫ 'Adi was published by one who for years was a resident of the city of Mosul.[34] This statement that Ibn Ḫallikan gives the biography of 'Adi is a fact that cannot be questioned; but that 'Adi founded the Yezidi sect is a theory that is by no means "generally agreed upon." Nor can it be substantiated. To justify this position, let me quote in full what the Arab biographer and two other Mohammedan scholars have to say on the problem.

1 What Ibn Ḫallikan has to say on Šeiḫ 'Adi:

"The Šeiḫ 'Adi Ibn Masafir Al-Hakkari was an ascetic, celebrated for the holiness of his life, and the founder of a religious order called after him Al-'Adawiah. His reputation spread to distant countries, and the number of his followers increased to a great multitude. Their belief in his sanctity was so excessive that, in saying their prayers, they took him for their ḳibla; and imagined that in the next life they would have in him their most precious treasure and their best support. Before this, he had as a disciple a great number of eminent šeiḫs and men remarkable for their holiness. He then retired from the world and fixed his residence among the mountains of the Hakkari, near Mosul, where he built a cell (or a monastery) and gained the favor of the people in that country to a degree unexampled in the history of the anchorites. It is said that the place of his birth was a village called Bait Far, situated in the province of

Baal-bek, and that the house in which he was born is still visited (as a place of sanctity). He died A. H. 557 (A. D. 1162), or as some say A. H. 555, in the town where he resided (in the Hakkari region). He was interred in the monastery that he had erected. His tomb is much frequented, being considered by his followers one of the most sacred spots to which a pilgrimage can be made. His descendants continue to wear the same distinctive attire as he did and to walk in his footsteps. The confidence placed in their merits is equal to that formerly shown to their ancestor, and like him they are treated with profound respect. Abu Ibarakat ibn Al-Mustawfi notices the Šeiḫ 'Adi in his history of Arbela, and places him in the list of those persons who visited that city. Muzaffar Ad-Din, the sovereign of Arbela, said that when a boy he saw the Šeiḫ 'Adi at Mosul. According to him, he was a man of medium size and tawny complexion; he related also many circumstances indicative of his great sanctity. The Šeiḫ died at the age of ninety years."[37]

2 What Mohammed-Amin-Al-'Omari has to say on Šeiḫ 'Adi:

"They say that the Šeiḫ 'Adi was one of the inhabitants of Ba'albek; that he transported himself to Mosul, and from thence to Jabal Laš, a dependency of this city (Mosul), where he resided until his death. They also say that he was from Ḥawran, and that his lineage goes back as far as Marwan bn al-Ḥakam, also that he is Šaraf ad Din Abou'l Faḍail 'Adi bn Masafir bn Isma'il bn Mousa bn Marwan bn al Ḥasan bn Marwan bn Mohammed bn Marwan bn al Ḥakam, who died in the ear 558. His grave, which is well known, is the object of pious pilgrimages."

"God tried him by a calamity, to wit, the appearance of a sect of apostates, called the Yezidis, because they claim to be descended from Yezid. They adore the sun and render worship to the devil. The following are some of the precepts of their faith that I found in a small tract made by one of the inhabitants of Aleppo, who knows their religion:

I. Adultery becomes lawful when committed by (mutual) consent.

II. They pretend that when the day of judgment comes, the šeiḫ 'Adi will put them into a wooden basin which he will place on his head in order to cause them to enter into Paradise while uttering these contemptuous words: 'I do this (or, I make them do this) by compelling God or in spite of him.'

III. The visit which they pay to the tomb of Šeiḫ 'Adi is for them a pilgrimage which the devotees accomplished no matter how far distant the country is that they inhabit, and without being concerned about the expenses that the journey carries with it."[88]

3 What Yasin Al-Hatib-al-Omari-Al-Mausili has to say on Šeiḫ 'Adi:

"In this year 557 died the saint and the pious devotee 'Adi bn Musafir, who performed miracles. His death took place in the city Hakkariya, one of the dependencies of Mosul. His origin is from Ba'albek, which he left in order to come to Mosul, that he might consecrate himself to God. He passed a solitary life on the mountains and in caverns where lions and other wild beasts visited him often."

"It is said that he was descended from the family of Omayyids, and this is the lineage which he attributed to himself: 'Adi bn Musafir bn Isma'il bn Mousa bn Marwan bn al-Ḥasan bn Marwan bn al-Ḥakam bn Al-'Ass bn Omayya."

"He was versed in the knowledge of the divine law. God tried him by a calamity by raising the Yezidis, who pretended that this Šeiḫ is God, and who have made his tomb the object of their pilgrimage. They arrive there every year at the sound of drums in order to give themselves to games and debauchery."

"The Christians of the land, and especially the partisans of the Nestorians are far from having the same opinion of the Šeiḫ 'Adi as have the Moslems or the Yezidis. The following passage which one reads in a Chaldean manuscript entitled 'Awarda'[39] and which I saw some time ago in the Church of Karmalis,[40] proves this sufficiently. This is the translation of the passage which I have extracted from a song composed by a bishop of Arbil, in honor of Rabban Hormuzd[41] and other saints, and in which the author makes mention of 'Adi in these terms:

"'Great misfortunes have followed, falling upon us; a formidable enemy came to torment us. He was a descendant of Hagar, the slave of our mother. This enemy who made our life unfortunate was a Mohammedan, called 'Adi. He deceived us by vile tricks, and has finished by taking possession of our riches and of our convent, which he consecrated to things that are illicit (to have a strange worship). An innumerable multitude of Mussulmen have attached themselves to him and have vowed to him a blind submission. The renown of his name, which is Šeiḫ 'Adi, has spread down to our days in all the cities of all the countries.' "[42]

These are the accounts which we have of Šeiḫ 'Adi in his relation to the Yezidis, and they deserve our special attention. For not only are the writers scholars of the highest authority, but they are to a certain extent eye-witness authorities. The last two are from the city of Mosul, which is the only city in the Mohammedan world whose widely spreading scholarship has acquired for it the name "Dar-al-'Ulum," *i. e.*, the home of sciences. Moreover, they come from a family whose members are known as 'Olama, highly intellectual, broad-minded Mohammedan gentlemen. While at Mosul, I had the honor of calling often on Ḥasan. Efendi al 'Omari, and especially on Suleiman Efendi al Omari. Ibn Ḫallikan as a trustworthy biographer needs no further introduction than the mere mentioning of his name. What adds to his reputation as a scholar is the fact that, being a resident of Arbila in the province of Mosul, he had at his command firsthand information.

Another noteworthy fact is that all three of these scholars agree in their account of Šeiḫ 'Adi, in their tracing of his genealogy, in describing him as the most perfect model of hermits, in praising him for his manner of life, which they regard as a life of holiness. They agree also in their definition of the common people's attitude toward the Šeiḫ: that he was deified and that his tomb has been made the object of pilgrimage. And finally they are silent about his supposed founding of the sect in question. There is no intimation that he was a heretic, or that he established such a schism. To be sure, Ibn Ḫallikan makes mention of a religious order which was called after the Šeiḫ's name, but he designates them as 'Adawia and not as Yezidis. This might have been such an order as the Brotherhood of Assanusi, called after Mohammed ibn 'Ali as-Sanusi, or as many other orders of dervishes and šeiḫs of mystical type, that have taken rise from time to time in the religious history of Islam. The other two speak of the appearance of the Yezidis, but they look at the incident as a calamity to the šeiḫ because they deified him and worshipped at his tomb. Their remarks tend to show that the Yezidi sect were known as such before the time of 'Adi; that their appellation was based on the pretension that they were descendants of Yesid; that they were apostates from Islam; that they were some of those who weer attached to 'Adi by reason of his wide reputation as a saint, and were led by their ignorance to take him for a god; and that they were worshippers of the sun and the devil. It is inconceivable to us, if we apply the principles of modern criticism to what we know of the character of the Mohammedan historians, that they should write the life of one who is responsible for the rise of a sect, the foundation of whose religion is the devil, and not curse him and the devil with him a hundred million times.

Such are the theories that have been advanced in the discussion relating to the religious origin of the Yezidi sect, and we have found not only that they are far from reaching the solution of the problem, but also that the method that they employ does not seem to be the proper one for solving such a question. The tradition of the Yezidis that they are descended from Yezid bn Mu'Awiya which has been accepted as the fact by some western scholars is only a myth, without historical justification. As to the Christian tradition, all that can tell us is that some Yezidis might have been at one time Christians; but as to who was the founder of the sect it gives us no light. Likewise, all that we can learn from the theory advocated by the second school is that some phases of the Persian religion might have survived with that of the devil-worshippers. We may admit, I think, that some Yezidis are Persian in their origin. But as to who was the originator of their religion this theory helps us not a whit. So also we have found that the relation of Šeiḫ 'Adi to this sect is not that of a founder. He is only one of many whom their ignorance led to class as deities.

IV

The Dogmatic View of Mohammedan Scholars

While the Yezidi myth regards the sect as descendants of Adam, of Yezid bn Mu awiya, or of a colony from the north, while the Christian tradition of the East traces them to a Christian origin, while among the western orientalists some say that they were founded by Yezid bn Mu awiya, others that they are of Persian origin, etc., the Mohammedan dogmatics, on the other hand, assert that they are *Murtaddoon,* that is, apostates from Islam. To understand the significance of this term, I must mention the several words used for those who are considered as infidels according to Mohammedan theology. *Kafir* is one who hides or denies the truth; *Mushrik* is one who ascribes companions to God; *Mulhid* is one who has deviated from the truth; *Zandik* is one who asserts his belief in the doctrine of dualism; *Munafik* is one who secretly disbelieves in the mission of Mohammed; *Dahri* is an atheist; *Watani* is a pagan or idolator; and finally *Murtadd* is one who apostasizes from Isalm. The Yezidis are put in the category of those who, after once accepting the religion of Islam, later rejected it.

One author, of those to whose writings I had access, in an explicit statement regards these people as apostates. I refer to Amin-al-'Omari-al Mausili (of Mosul). After praising Šeiḫ 'Adi, the Mosulian goes on to say, "God tried him (*i. e.*, 'Adi) by a calamity, to wit, the appearance of Al-Murtaddoon, called the Yezidis because they pretended to have been descended from Yezid."[43]. Another Mohammedan scholar that mentions these people is Yasin Al-Ḫatib-al-'Omari-al Mausili. Writing on Šeiḫ 'Adi, and praising him as the former writer does, he says, "He was versed in the knowledge of the divine law. God tried him by a calamity by raising up the Yezidis, who pretend that this Šeih is God, and who have made his tomb the object of their pilgrimage."[44]

While these authors throw some light on the subject that the sect in question derives its appellation from a historic person, they leave us entirely in the dark as to who that person was, as the Arab historians mention many prominent men who bore the name Yezid.

This obscurity regarding the person of the founder of the sect is made clear by one whose work is equally, if not more, authoritative than that of any other Mohammedan scholar on matters pertaining to religious and philosophical sects. This authority is Mohammed Aš-Šahrastani. He is the only Mohammedan writer that I could reach that, in a clear language, traces this most interesting sect to its founder.

"The Yezidis are the followers of Yezid bn Unaisa, who [said that he] kept friendship with the first Muhakkama before the Azariḳa, and he separated himself from those who followed after them with the exception of Al-Abaḍia, for with these he kept friendship. He believed that God would send an apostle from among the Persians and would reveal to him a book that is already written in heaven, and would reveal the whole (book) to him at one time,[45] and as a result he would leave the law of Mohammed, the Chosen One, may God bless and save him!—and follow the religion of the Sabians mentioned in the Koran. But these are not the Sabians who are found in Ḥaran and Wasit. But Yezid kept friendship with the people of the book who recognized the Chosen One as a prophet, even though they did not accept his (Mohammed's) religion. And he said that the followers of the ordinances are among those who agree with him; but that others are hiding the truth and give companions to god and that every sin, small or great, is idolatry.[46]

It is clear, then, that Aš-Šahrastani finds the religious origin of this interesting people in the person of Yezid bn Unaisa. He calls them his *Aseḥab, i. e.*, his followers, a term by which he designates the relation between a sect and its originator. Al-Ḥaraṯiyah he describes as "Aseḥab al-Hareṯ," and "Al Ḥafeziyah Aseḥab Hafez," and so on. We are to understand, therefore, that to the knowledge of the writer, bn Unaisa is the founder of the Yezidi sect, which took its name from him.

Mohammed Aš-Šahrastani states also, in a logical way, the theological views of the head of the Yezidis. Yezid, he says, is on the positive side, in sympathy with the first Muḥakkamah before the Azariḳa. Now, the first Muhakkamah is an appellative applied to the Muslim schismatics called Al-Ḫawarij, because they disallowed the judgment of the Hakaman, *i. e.*, the two judges, namely 'Abd Mousa al-Aš-'Aree and Am ibn-al-'As; and said that judgment belongs only to God. And Al-Azariḳa were a heretical Muslim sect called Al-Ḫawarij or Ḥeroriyah, so named in relation to Nafi' ibn-Al-Azraḳ. They asserted that 'Ali committed an act of infidelity by submitting his case to arbitration, and that the slaying of him by Ibn Muljama was just; and they declare that the companions (of the Prophet) were guilty of infidelity. Yezid moreover, is said to have been in sympathy with Al-Abaḍiyah, a sect founded by 'Abd-Allah ibn Ibad, who taught that if a man commits a kabirah or great sin he is an infidel and not a believer.

It is evident, therefore, that according to this exposition the Yezid in question was one of Al-Ḫawarij, and their principle is expressly attributed to him: every sin, small or great, is idolatry. According to this it might be inferred that the Yezidis were originally a Ḫarijite sub-sect. They still hold to the Ḫarijite principle. (Cf. their position to the Ottoman Government, pp. 71-74). As we said some Mohammedan writers other than Ashahr-Astani also (pp. 118-119) regard them as apostate Moslems, Aš-Šahrastani himself classes them with the Moslem heretics. Now Al-Ḫawarij were the first to rebel against 'Ali at Ḥaroora, a certain suburb of Al-Koofa, from which it is distant two miles. They are called also Al-Ḥeroriyah, because they first assembled there and accepted the doctrine that government belongs only to God. And one sect of Al-Ḥawarij was An-Nâṣibiyah who made it a matter of religious obligation to bear a violent hatred to 'Ali. Such is the place of bn Unaisa among the Moslem heretics, but this is only one side of his religious system."

There is another side to Yezid's doctrine. He held that God would send an apostle from Persia, to whom he would reveal a book already written in heaven. This apostle was to be an opponent of the prophet of Islam in that he would leave Mohammed's religion and follow that of the Ṣabians mentioned in the Koran. These are referred to by Mohammed, together with the Christians and the Jews, in three different places in the Book. One such reference is in Surah 2, 59: "They who believe as well as Jews, Christians and Sabeans, whoever believeth in God and in the Last Day, and do that which is right, shall have their reward with their Lord."

Surah 5, 73, also:

"They who believe as well as Jews, Christians and Sabeans, whoever of them believe in God and the Last Day, and do what is right, on them shall no fear come; neither shall they be put to grief."

And Surah 22, 17:

"They who believe as well as Jews, Sabeans and Christians and the Magians, and those who join gods with God, verily God shall decide between them on the Day of Resurrection."

In these passages Mohammed seems to regard the Sabians of the Koran as believers in the true God and in the resurrection. And in Surah 22, 17, he seems to distinguish them from Magians and polytheists. Hence, we are to infer that the Apostle of whom Yezid bn Unaisa says that he will come from the land of the 'Ajam (Persian), will identify himself with the religion of the Ṣabians. This implies that he will believe in the true God and in the Day of Resurrection. But from some Arab writers we learn more of these Ṣabian beliefs than the Prophet of Islam has mentioned. According to some the Ṣabians were a sect of unbelievers who worshipped the stars secretly, and openly professed to be Christians. According to others, they were of the religion of Ṣabi, the son of Seth, the son of Adam; while others said they resembled the Christians, except that their *ḳiblah* was toward the South, from whence the wind blows. In the *Kamûs* it is said that they were of the religion of Noah. Al-Baiḍawi says that some assert that they were worshippers of angels, and that others say that they are the worshippers of stars. Al-Bertuni[48] calls the Manichaeans of Samarḳand Sabians. Bar Hebraeus[49] asserts that the religion of the Sabians is the same as that of the ancient Chaldeans. In commenting on Surah 2, 59, Zamaḫšari (Al-Keššaf) says that the name Ṣabian comes from a root meaning one who has departed from one religion to another religion, and that the Ṣabians were those who departed from Judaism and Christianity and worshipped angels. On this same verse, Šams Ad-Din Mohammed Al-Ḥarrani (Jami Al-Bijan fi Tafsir Al-Koran) says: "The Ṣabians, *i. e.*, those who departed from one religion to another religion, stood between the Magians and the Jews and the Christians without having any revealed religion of their own. According to some they were people of the Book; according to others they were worshippers of angels; while others say, they believed in one God but followed no Prophet." This same commentator on Surah 5, 73, says: "The Ṣabians were a Christian sect; some say that they were worshippers of angels; others assert that they worshipped God alone, but had no revealed religion." On this same verse Zamaḫšari remarks, "The Ṣabians were those who departed from all religions."

Now what Mohammed Aš-Šahrastani really means by the Ṣabians of the Koran, I am unable to state. In his general discussion of Ṣabianism however (vol. 2, pp. 201-250), he seems to speak of two main Ṣabian sects. He refers to one together with the ancient philosophers; and declares that the Ṣabians followed rational ordinances and judgments which originally they may have derived from some prophetic authority, but that they denied all prophecy. The philosophers followed their own devices and took their system from no prophetic source. The authority we are quoting calls this sect "the original Ṣabian sect," and says that it followed Seth and Enoch. In another place (vol. 1, p. 24) he writes, "The Jews and the Christians follow a revealed Book; the Magians and the Manichæans, a like Book; the original Ṣabian sect, ordinances and judgments, but accepts no Book; the original philosophers, the atheists, the star-worshippers, the idol-worshippers, and the Brahmans believe in none of these."

The other main Ṣabian sect is mentioned together with the Jews, the Christians, and the Moslems. The difference between these religious bodies, according to Aš-Šahrastani, is that "the Ṣabians do not follow the Law (of God) or Islam; the Christians and the Jews believe in these, but do not accept the Law (religion) of Mohammed; while the Moslems believe in them all.

Aš-Šahrastani, moreover, derives the name Ṣabian (p. 203) from a root meaning one who turns aside, deviates; and declares that the Ṣabians were those who turned aside from the statutes of God), and deviated from the path of the prophets. He seems to regard the notion that man is incapable of approaching God, and that therefore he is in constant need of intercessors and mediators, as a controlling idea in Ṣabianism. This belief, the writer points out, has manifested itself in three different forms: in the veneration of angels among what he calls the followers of angels; the adoration of stars among the followers of stars; and in the worship of idols among the followers of idols, heathens (pp. 203, 244). The last two, we are told, are polytheists, and referred to in the Koranic statement:

("When Abraham said to his father, Azar, 'Dost thou take idols for gods?'—Surah 6, 74. Said he—Abraham—'Do ye serve what ye hew out?'—Surah 37, 93. When he—Abraham—said to his father, 'Oh my sir! why dost thou worship what can neither hear nor see nor avail thee aught?'—Surah 19, 43.")

And in the following references:

("And when the night overshadowed him he saw a star and said, 'This is my Lord.' And when he saw the moon beginning to rise he said, 'This is my Lord.' And when he saw the sun beginning to rise he said, 'This is my Lord, this is greatest of all.' ")—Surah 6, 76, 77, 78.

But Mohammed Aš-Šahrastani makes mention of another Ṣabian sect which he names Al-Ḫarbâniyah (pp. 248–250). Its distinctive feature, he says, is the belief that the Creator indwelleth in other beings. They held that God is one in his essence, but many in his appearances. He dwells in the seven planets, and in the earthly beings that are rational, good, and excellent in righteousness. Human body is his temple; he may abide within it and live and move as a man. He is too good, we read, to create anything evil. God is the source of good, and evil is either an accidental and necessary thing, or related to the evil source. They believed also, our authority informs us, in the transmigration of souls, and taught that the Resurrection of which the prophets had spoken was only the end of one generation and the beginning of another here on earth. This doctrine, the Mohammedan critics affirm, is alluded to in the passages:

("Does he promise you that when ye are dead, and have become dust and bones, that then ye will be brought forth? Away, away with what ye are promised,—there is only our life in the world! We die and we live and we shall not be raised.")—Surah 23, 37–39.

Now I cannot say which of the Ṣabian sects are those that "are mentioned in the Koran," which Yezid bn Unaisa says, the Persian Apostle will follow; nor can I say which are those that "are found in Ḥarran and Wasit." One thing, however, is clear: according to Aš-Šahrastani the Ṣabians of the Koran differ in their faith from those of Ḥarran. The Harranians were remnants of the old heathen of Mesopotamia; they were polytheistic, and star-worship had the chief place in their religion, as in the worship of the older Babylonian and Syrian faiths. They were regarded as such by the Mohammedans, so that under Al-Mamûn, they sheltered themselves under the name, Ṣabians, that they might be entitled to the toleration which the Ṣabians of the Koran have because they were considered among the people of the Book.[50] Another thing to be noticed is that there is a close resemblance between the belief of the Ṣabian sect which Aš-Šahrastani calls Al-Ḥarbaniyah and that of the Yezidi sect.

Such is, in the main, the religion of the Persian

Apostle and is logically the religion of Yezid bn Unaisa which announces the coming of such a messenger. We may conclude, therefore, that the founder of the Yezidi sect believed in God and in the Day of Resurrection; that he, perhaps, honored the angels and the stars, and that he was neither polytheistic nor a true believer in the Prophet of Islam. This last point is referred to also explicitly in the statement quoted, that Yezid associated himself with those of the people of the Book who recognized Mohammed as a prophet though they did not become his followers. This is the negative aspect, so to speak, of bn Unaisa's religious views. He is also said to have claimed that the followers of the ordinances[51] agreed with him. This statement tends to indicate that he might have accepted some phases of the Muslim faith. And the fact that he belonged to *Al-Hawarij* implies that he was one of those who were "condemning and rejecting 'Ali for his scandalous crime of parleying with Muawiya, the first of the Omayyid line, and submitting his claims to arbitration." Such are in brief the fundamental elements in the religious system of one who may be held responsible for the rise of the sect in question.

There can be no doubt, it seems to me, that the Yezidis are the followers of Yezid bn Unaisa. The statement of our authority, Mohammed Aš-Šahrastani (see pp. 119-120), is so clear that it can bear no other interpretation. And what is far more important, it comes from the pen of one who is considered of the highest authority among the Arab scholars on questions relating to philosophical and religious sects. In his bibliographical work Ibn Ḫallikan speaks of his profound scholarship in the highest terms: "Aš-Šahrastani, a dogmatic theologian of the 'Ašarite sect, was distinguished as an Imam and a doctor of the law. He displayed the highest abilities as a jurisconsult. The Kitab al-Milal wa n-Niḥal (treatise on religions and sects) is one of his works on scholastic theology. He remained without an equal in that branch of science." Now, Mohammed Aš-Šahrastani (A. H. 467–549) A. D. 1074–1133 was a contemporary of 'Adi (A. H. 465–555) A. D. 1072–1162, yet he makes no allusion to him when he refers to the rise of this most interesting sect; nor does he make mention of any other supposed founder except the one he records. For these reasons I accept the historical assertion of this distinguished author.

I am of the opinion, therefore, that the Yezidis received their name from Yezid bn Unaisa, their founder as a kharijite sub sect in the early period of Islam; that, attracted by Šeiḫ 'Adi's reputation, they joined his movement and took him for their chief religious teacher; that in the early history of the sect and of 'Adi many Christians, Persians, and Moslems united with it; and that large survivals or absorptions of pagan beliefs or customs are to be found in modern Yezidism. In other words the actual religion of the Yezidis is syncretism in which it is easy to recognize

Yezidi, Christian, Moslem, especially sufism and pagan elements.

Like the master they believe in the true God and in the Resurrection, honor the angels and the stars, disbelieve in the mission of Mohammed and ignore 'Ali, regard every sin, small or great, as idolatry or infidelity, and expect the appearance of a prophet from Persia. The fact of their connection with such a religious leader explains the reason why they are hated by both the Sunnites and the Shiites. The followers of bn My'awiya can only be despised by the latter; but the believer such a heretical one as the son of Unaisa are necessarily condemned by the former also. For he was, as I have already stated, anti-Mohammed and anti-'Ali. And it is worth remembering also that the fourth Calif is more honored among the Moslems of Persia than his son Ḥusein is; and consequently any contemptuous attitude toward the father will give rise to more bitter feeling on the part of his followers than the murder of the son would occasion.

There is one question, however, which does not appear to be very easy to answer; namely, how the Yezidis came to trace their origin to Yezid bn Mu-'awiya and not to Yezid bn Unaisa. Three explanations may be given. One is that their ignorance led them to mistake the former for the latter, as they have identified many of their šeiḫs with angels and deities. Among ignorant people, as these are, without record and without any one who can read, the occasion of such an error is not strange. Another answer is that they intentionally made the identification in order to escape the persecution of the Sunnites, among whom most of them lived. Though specious, this idea is not tenable, for it is not their habit to deny their origin for the sake of safety. Even in that case, they would still be hated by the Shiites. The third theory is that they have a notion that they are descended from a noble personage, and the second Calif being such a personage, their ignorance led them to take him for their founder. And the identity of the two names, of course, helped much toward the formation of the legend.

It is to be noticed that the religion of this Yezid contained, from its inception, a fundamental doctrine which appealed to the pagans of Persia more than it did to Al-jahaleen of Arabia. In its very structure it insulted the latter country by despising its prophet. On the other hand, it expressed its sympathy with a prophet from Persia and with his religion. This declaration magnified Persia and its inhabitants and gave them preëminence, thereby making an impression on the attitude of the people toward Yezidism. Therefore they looked on it not as a foreign but as a native cult. The entertaining of such a view, consequently, led many fire, or devil-worshippers and the followers of Zoroastrianism to embrace the new religion (Al-mašrik, vol. 2, p. 35). And if the predicted teacher arose, we can imagine the great success which he must have had among his countrymen.

This fact not only accounts for the existence of traces of old Persian religion, but it gives the reason why the Kurdish predominates over the Arab element in Yezidism.

The new sect appears to have existed as a very loose organization after the death of its founder: this looseness put them in a condition to follow any one who would exhibit some qualifications for leadership. Therefore, when they heard about 'Adi they naturally flocked to him. And it is very likely that, entertaining the idea of a coming prophet as they still do, they might have thought him the promised one. What might have added to the confirmation of this notion was his fame as a saint, to whom a number of miracles were attributed. Even the lions and the serpents which lived in his neighborhood and paid him frequent visits were endowed, it is said, with supernatural sweetness.

From what we know of 'Adi's movement, we have sufficient reason to conclude that many Moslems and Christians followed him. The historians of both faiths bear witness to the fact that 'Adi's reputation was widespread, and that people of every condition followed him (see pp. 111-115). The Nestorian bishop of Arbela, whom Yasin Al-'Omari quotes (see p. 114) asserts that innumerable multitudes flocked to him, deplores the situation of the Christian church resulting from this uprising, and complains of the possession by the Šeiḫ of a monastery belonging to his denomination. Moreover, as has been shown, there exist among the Yezidis certain Moslem and Christian practices which cannot be accounted for on any other ground, since, so far as we know their character, they make no compromise in matters of religion.

Not only Yezidi, Persian, Moslem, and Christian elements are to be found in modern Yezidism, but there are many remains of the old pagan religions which find expression in the devil-worshippers of to-day. Such is the notion of the sacredness of the number seven, an idea which belongs to the common stock of the ancient inhabitants of Mesopotamia. The Yezidis have seven sanjaks, each has seven burners; their cosmogany shows that God created seven angels or gods; their principal prayer is the appeal to God through seven šeiḫs; the sceptre engraved on the front of the temple of their great saint has seven branches. This reminds us at once of the Ṣabians who adored seven gods or angels who directed the course of seven planets; the seven days of the week were dedicated to their respective deities. Moreover, we note in the Babylonian-Assyrian poem, the seven gates through which Ištar descended to the land without return. Likewise, the number seven played an important part in the religious system of Israel.

Further, like the Ḥarranians, the modern *Satan-parast* worship the sun and the moon at their rising and setting. The sun was worshipped also in Canaan, I Sam. 6: 9. The horses of the sun were worshipped in the temple at Jerusalem, II Kings 25: 5, 11. The worship of the host of heaven (the sun, the moon, the planets), were found in Judea. In Babylon, there were at least two shrines to sun-god Šamas, one at Sippar, and ther other at Larsa.

Other survivals of the ancient religions found in Yezidism are the worship of birds (see p. 150); the special importance attached to the New Year because of its bearing on individual welfare by reason of the good or evil decision of the gods rendered them (see pp. 46, 174); and the belief in occurrences of nuptials in the heavens (see p. 174).

Moreover, many religious beliefs of the Pre-Islamic Arabs survive among the modern Yezidis. Such is the belief in sacred wells in connection with sanctuaries found in all parts of the Semitic region, the most conspicuous of which is that of Mecca. Gifts were cast into this holy water of Zamzam, as they were cast into the sacred wells of other places. When the grandfather of Mohammed 'Abd Al-Muttalib cleaned out the well, he found two golden gazelles and a number of swords. The water of such holy springs was believed to possess healing power, and was carried home by pilgrims, as the water of Zamzam now is (Yaḳut I, 434).[52] An impure person, furthermore, dared not approach the sacred waters. A woman in her uncleanness was afraid for her children's sake to bathe in the holy water at the sanctuary of Dusares. According to Ibn Hišam "A woman who adopts Islam breaks with the heathen god by purifying herself in this pool." This was taken to mean that her act was a breach of the ritual of the spot. And all the pilgrims changed their clothes when they entered the sacred precinct.[53]

Another common heathen practice in the time of Al-jahliya was the worship of holy trees. According to Tabari there was a date-palm tree at Nejran. It was adored at an annual feast, when it was hung all around with fine clothes and women's ornaments. A similar tree to which the people of Mecca resorted annually, and hung upon it weapons, garments, ostriches' eggs, and other things, is spoken of in the tradition of the prophet under the name of "dhat anwat," or "tree to hang things on."[54] The Goddess Al-'Ozza was believed to reside in a tree. According to Yaḳut (III, 261), the tree at Hadaibiya, mentioned in the Koran (sura XLVIII, 18) was visited by pilgrims who expected to derive a blessing from it, till it was cut down by the Calif Omar lest it should be worshipped like Al-Lat and Al-'Ozza. It was considered deadly to pluck a twig from such sacred trees.

The prevalence of stone-worship is another sign of paganism existing before Islam, and noteworthy is the theory advanced by the Mohammedan writers to account for its origin. According to Ibn Hišam[55] the beginning of this idolatry was that "the Meccans when their land became too narrow for them spread abroad over the country, and all took stones from their sanctuary, the Kaaba, out of reverence for their temple, and they set them up whenever they formed a settlement; and they walked around them as they used to go about the Holy House. This led them at last to worship every stone that pleased their fancy."

It is to be noticed, furthermore, that poly-demonism, *i. e.*, the belief in divine powers, in spirits, is the most characteristic feature of the old nomad religions. Many traces of this belief have been preserved in the Old Testament, and also in the popular religion of the Syria and Palestine of to-day. There are many instances in the Old Testament of the belief in divine powers inhabiting springs, trees, stones. We may refer to the sacred wells at Ḳadeš (Gen. 14: 7) and at Beeršeba (Gen. 21, 28, 30, 31); to the sacred oracular tree at Shekem (Gen. 12, 6; Deut. 11, 3); to the sacred stone of Bethel, which gave the place its name, as it is called "a house of God" (Gen. 28, 22).[56]

Now, the traces of all these religious beliefs are found in modern Yezidism. In connection with the temple of Šeiḫ 'Adi, there is a sacred spring, and there are similar ones in different parts of the Yezidi districts. The water of these springs is held to have healing power, and is carried by pilgrims to their homes. In these pools, especially in that of 'Adi's, the Yezidis cast coins, jewelry, and other presents, which, they think, the chief saint takes from time to time; and to this day no one may enter the holy valley with its sacred fountain, unless he first purify his body and clothes.[57] The devil-worshippers adore, likewise, sacred trees. They make pilgrimages to them, hang things on them, and entertain the belief that whoever unties or shakes off a shred of cloth will be afflicted with disease. Again, the Yezidis kiss the stones that satisfy their imagination, and make vows to them (see pp. 41, 50). Nor is this all. The shouting of the Yezidi pilgrims, as they reach the sacred territory, and the noisy ceremony of their ḥajj, with its dancing[58] and its excitement—a rite which has brought against them all sorts of accusations[59] —are nothing but the remnants of Pre-Islamic paganism.[60]

Such, then, are the steps which the religion of Yezid took before it came to shape itself into its present form. It is made up of five different elements, pagan, that contributed by the founder, Persian, Mohammedan, and Christian. Does not such a state of affairs find a historical parallel in some other religions? Take, for example, Christianity. In it we find that the distinctive characteristics of the founder have been wrapped up in many foreign elements brought in by those who came from other religions.

NOTES ON CHAPTER I

[1] This may be traced to the Mohammedan myth that when the primal pair fell from their estate of bliss in the heavenly Paradise, Adam landed on a mountain in Ceylon and Eve fell at Jiddah, on the western coast of Arabia. After a hundred years of wandering, they met near Meccah, and here Allah constructed for them a tabernacle, on the site of the present Kaaba, S. M. Zwemer, *Arabia*, p. 17; Aš-Šahrastani, II, 430.

[2] Anistase: *Al-Mašrik*, vol. 2, p. 33.

[3] Cf. p. 35.

[4] Cf. p. 34.

[5] Cf. p. 37.

[6] *Al-Mašrik*, vol. 2, p. 33.

[7] Scottish Geog. Mag., vol. 14, p. 295.

[8] Layard: *Nineveh and Its Remains*, vol. II, p. 254.

[9] Layard: *Nineveh and Babylon*, p. 94.

[10] S. G. M., vol. 14, p. 300.

[11] Fraser: *Mesopotamia and Persia*, p. 287.

[12] Fraser: Ibid, p. 147.

[13] Rich: *Residence in Kurdistan*, vol. II, p. 69.

[14] *Al-Mašrik*, vol. II, p. 396.

[15] Ibid, vol. III, p. 493.

[16] Fraser: Ibid; Rich, ibid.

[17] Badger: *Nestorians and Their Rituals*, vol. I, p. 111; Fraser, ibid, p. 285.

[18] *Al-Mašrik*, ibid, p. 36.

'Abdišū was at one time bishop of Sinjar; cf. Fardaisa de 'Eden, ed. by B. Cardaḥi, Beirut, 1889, p. 5.

[19] Ibid, pp. 56, 110, 832.

[20] Ibid. This rite is practiced by the Yezidis of Ḥalitiyeh, a dependency of Darbeker, where the Yezidis are few in number.

[21] Southgate: *A Tour Through Armenia,* etc., vol. II, p. 179.

[22] See p. 42 of this book. Badger, ibid, p. 128.

[23] I mean by the philosophical method the attempt to prove certain assumption by theorizing, and by the historical method the endeavor to verify a theory by obtaining data from historical sources. The former method is based on speculation; the latter on historical inquiry.

[24] The Enc. of Mission, p. 797. In his letter to me of date August 6, 1907, the Rev. A. N. Andrus, of Mardin, says: "The Yezidis may be related in religious cult with the Guebres of India."

[25] Muir: *Life of Mohammed,* vol. IV, p. 151.

[26] Fraser: ibid, p. 205.

[27] Badger, ibid, p. 129.

[28] S. G. M., vol. 14.

[29] Eugene Bore: *Dict. des Religions,* T. IV, *Art. Yezidis,* Southgate, ibid, p. 317.

[30] Fraser, ibid, p. 289.

[31] Jackson: *Persia, Past and Present,* p. 10: J. A. O. S., 25, p. 178, New Int. Enc. "Yezidis."

[32] H. Poincaré: *Science and Hypothesis.* Trans., G. B. Halsted, p. 5 seq.

[33] The fact that the importance of the method of comparative religion has been generally recognized in the scientific world has led to the danger of rushing into the other extreme of paying attention exclusively to points of similarity and resemblance, and of entirely disregarding, or at any rate thrusting into the background as unimportant that which is dissimilar.

[34] Southgate, ibid, p. 317; Jackson, J. A. O. S., vol. XXV, p. 171.

[35] Victor Dingelstedt, S. G. M., vol. XIV, p. 295.

[36] Siouffi, who was for about twenty years a French vice-consul in Mosul.

[37] Ibn Ḥallikan, vol. I, p. 316.

[38] Manhal Al-Uliya wa Mašrab-ul-Asfia, "Šeiḫ 'Adi," quoted by M. N. Siouffi, Journal Asiatique, 1885, p. 80.

[39] Warda, "the rose," is the name of a collection of hymns composed by George Warda (1224 A. D.), Bishop of Arbila; cf. Bar Hebraeus, Chron. Eccl., vol. II, p. 402. Warda is one of the most conspicuous writers of hymns in the thirteenth century which was the age of song with the Nestorian church. His poems have entered so largely into the use of the Nestorian church that one of their service books is to this day called the Warda; Badger, *The Nestorians,* vol. II, p. 25. Some of his hymns speak of the calamities of the years 1224–1227. A few specimens are given by Cardaḥi in *Liber Thesauri,* p. 51. Badger has translated one in his *Nestorians,* vol. II, pp. 51-57. Warda's poems have been edited by Heinrich Hilgenfeld, *Ausgewählte Gesänge des Giworgis Warda von Arbil,* Leipzig, 1904, and by Manna, Mosul, 1901.

[40] The village Karmalis is about twelve miles distant from Mosul, and is inhabited by Chaldeans, that is, Romanized Nestorians.

[41] Rabban Hormusd is a Chaldean monastery at Alkoš, a village about twenty miles north of Mosul.

[42] Al-Der-Al-Makn'un fi-l-Miater Al-Maḍiyat min Al-Ḳerun, "Šeiḫ 'Adi," quoted by M. N. Siouffi, Journal Asiatique, 1885, p. 81.

Yaḳut (vol. IV, p. 374) also regards Šeiḥ 'Adi an orthodox Mohammedan; "Šeiḫ 'Adi bn Musafir Aš-Šafe'e, šeiḫ of the Kurds and their Imam." 'Adi's orthodoxy is seen also in his writing. He wrote

'Itikad Ahl Al-Sunna "Belief of the Sunnites," the Wasaya "Consuls to the Cailifs," and two odds both of them mystic in their conception. They are all preserved in the Berlin Library; cf. Clement Huart, *History of Arabic Literature*, p. 273.

[43] Manhal-al-Uliya wa Mašrab ul Asfiya, "Šeih 'Adi," quoted by M. N. Siouffi, Journal Asiatique, 1885, p. 80.

[44] Al-Der-Al-Maknun fi-l-Miater Al-Madiyat min Al-Kerûn, "Šeih 'Adi," quoted by M. N. Siouffi, Journal Asiatique, 1885, p. 81.

[45] Contrary to Mohammed to whom, according to Moslem belief, the Koran was revealed at intervals.

[46] Kitab Al-Milal wa n-Nihal, vol. I, p. 101 seq. Harran was a city in the north of Mesopotamia, and southeast of Edessa, at the junction of the Damascus road with the highway from Nineveh to Carchamish. The moon-god had a temple in Harran, which enjoyed a high reputation as a place of pilgrimage. The city retained its importance down to the time of the Arab ascendency, but it is now in ruins. Yakut (vol. II, p. 331) says: "It was the home of Sabians; that is, the Harranians who are mentioned by the authors of Kutub Al-Milal wa n-Nihal." As to Wasit this same Yakut (vol. IV, p. 881) mentions about twenty different places bearing this name. The most prominent one is that built by Al-Hajjaj in 83 A. H. It is called Wasit "the intermediate" because it was situated midway between Kufa and Basrah. Another place Yakut (p. 889) mentions is Wasit ul-Rakkat, a town on the western side of the Euphrates, and about two days' journey from Harran. Perhaps this is the Wasit that Aš-Šahrastanî means.

[47] On these sects. See Aš-Šahrastanî, ibid, vol. II, pp. 85, 87, 89, 100 (42). His history, ed. Sachau, Leibzig, 1878, p. 207.

[49] At-Tarih, ed. Alton Salhanî, Beîrut, p. 266.

[50] Fihrist, p. 320. The Arabs used to call the Prophet Aṣ-ṣabi, because he departed from the religion of the Koreish to Al-Islam; cf. Al-Keššaf on Surah XXII, 17.

[51] Hudud, pl. of Hadad, restrictive ordinances, or statutes, of God respecting things lawful and things unlawful. The Hudud of God are of two kinds: First, those ordinances respecting eatables, drinkables, marriage, etc., what are lawful thereof and what are unlawful. Second, castigations, or punishments, prescribed, or appointed, to be inflicted upon him who does that which he has been forbidden to do. The first kind are called Hudud because they denote limits which God has forbidden to transgress; the second, because they prevent one's committing again those acts for which they are appointed as punishments, or because the limits thereof are determined. See Lane's Arabic Dictionary in Loco.

[52] Cf. also W. R. Smith, *Religion of the Semites,* p. 167. and D. B. Stade's *Biblische Theologie des Alten Testaments,* pp. 111 and 290.

[53] R. Smith, ibid, p. 49; cf. Ex. 3: 5, "And he said, Draw not nigh hither; put off thy shoes from off thy feet, for the place whereon thou standest is holy ground"; and Josh. 5: 15, "And the captain of the Lord's host said unto Joshua: Loose thy shoe from off thy feet, for the place whereon thou standest is holy. And Joshua did so."

In idolatrous days the Arabs did not wear any clothing in making the circuit of the Kaaba. In Islam, the orthodox way is as follows: Arrived within a short distance of Mecca, the pilgrims put off their ordinary clothing and assume the garb of a hajjee. Sandals may be worn but not shoes, and the head must be left uncovered. In Mandeanism, each person as he or she enters the Miškana, or tabernacle, disrobes, and bathes in the little circular reservoir. On emerging from the water, each one robes him or herself in the rasta, the ceremonial white garment.—*The London Standard*, Oct. 19, 1894." Prayer Meeting of the Starworshippers.

[64] Cf. R. Smith, ibid, p. 185, and Stade, ibid, p. 111 seq.

[65] Weil's translation, p. 39.

[66] Cf. R. Smith, ibid, pp. 203–212; S. I. Curtiss' *Primitive Semitic Religion To-day*, pp. 84–89; Stade, ibid, p. 114, seq.; see also II Sam. 5: 24, and John 5: 2, 3.

The original idea might have been that the waters, the stones, and the trees themselves were divinities. In Jud. 5: 21, we have the statement: "The river Kishon swept them away, that ancient river, the river Kishon." Now Kais was the name of an Arabian god in Pre-Islamic time. In Num. 5: 17 seq., an accused woman is tested by a sacred water. In Deut. 32: 4, "He is the rock," "rock" is as much a term for God as El, or elohim; cf. verses 15, 18, 30, 31; II Sam. 23: 3. In Ps. 18: 2, the word rock is used of God, "the Lord is my rock." Jacob took the stone which he had put under his head as a pillow, and raised it up as a pillar, poured oil upon it and called it the "house of God," Gen. 28: 18, 19, 22. "The sound of a going in the tops of the mulberry trees" (II Sam. 5: 24), for which David was to wait, was nothing less than the divine voice speaking to David in accordance with ancient conceptions.

[67] Layard: *Nineveh and Its Remains*, vol. I, p. 280.

[58] Dancing might have been also a religious ceremony in the Pre-Kanaanitic religion of Israel.

[59] The people in the East are under the impression that the Yezidis violate the law of morality during their festivals. According to Hurgronje (vol. 2, pp. 61–64, immorality is practised also in the sacred mosque of Mecca. This practice may be a survival of the institution of Kadeshes, who offered themselves in honor of the Deity in the sacred places where license usually prevailed during the festivals (Gen. 38: 21, and Deut. 23: 18).

[60] Cf. R. W. Smith, ibid, p. 432.

CHAPTER II

The Essential Elements in Yezidism

Although comparatively few in number, ignorant, and practically without a literature of any sort, the followers of Yezid are not without definitely formulated doctrines of faith which bind them together as a sect, and distinguish them from every other religious body. They cherish two fundamental beliefs. They believe in a deity of the first degree, God; and in a deity of the second degree, who, they seem to think, is composed of three persons in one, Melek Ṭâ'ûs, Šeiḫ 'Adi and Yezid.[1]

I

The Yezidi View of God

It is not easy to discover whether the conception of God, which exists to-day among the Yezidis, however shadowy, has come from Mohammedan or Christian sources, or whether it comes from that primitive stage where the worship of God and of inferior deities exists side by side. One thing, however, is apparent, and that is that the Yezidi notion of God does not seem to be influenced by any "positive religion" which traces its origin to the teachings of a great religious founder, who spoke as the organ of a divine revelation, and deliberately departed from the traditional religion. The Yezidis' idea of God is rather an image left on their mind than the result of any reflection. Hence, simple as it is, this conception is not so easy to define. The notion, so prominent in Greek philosophy, of God as an existence absolute and complete in himself, unchangeable, outside of time and space, etc., is unknown in Yezidi theology. So also the theocratic conception of Jehovah in Judaism is foreign to the dogma of this sect. Not even the Mohammedan idea of God as an absolute ruler, and the distinctive notion which the Christians have of God as Christ-like in character, are to be found in the religion of the devil-worshippers. And we have accustomed ourselves to think of the Supreme Being in these conventional terms. There is one element, however, which may be traced to Judaism, Christianity and Islam, namely, the belief in a personal God. But Yezidism holds that this deity is only the creator of the universe and not its sustainer. Its maintenance, according to this system, is left to the seven gods. Another element which may be said to be a remnant of some other religions is the idea of a transcendent God. But in this point, as in the other, the notion of transcendentalism in the religion of the devil-worshippers is not of the same degree as that of the other religions. The former conceives of the Almighty as retiring far away, and as having nothing to do with the affairs of the world, except once a year, on New Year's day, when he sits on his throne, calls the gods unto him, and delivers the power into the hands of the the god who is to descend to the earth. To sum up, the Yezidis' conception of a personal God is transcendental and static of the extreme type. In this it resembles somewhat the Platonic idea of the absolute. They call God in the Kurdish Khuda, and believe that he manifested himself in three different forms; in the form of a bird, Melek Ṭâ'ûs; in the form of an old man, Seiḫ 'Adi; and in the form of a young man, Yezid. They do not seem to offer him a direct prayer or sacrifice.

II

The Deity of the Second Degree

1. Melek Ṭâ'ûs

A distinguished modern scholar (see the printed text, p. 80, lines 12-35) argues that Ṭâ'ûs is the god Tammuz. His argument is that the word Ṭâ'ûs must embody an ancient god, but owing to the obscurity in which the origin of Yezidism and the being of Melek Ṭâ'ûs are wrapped, it is very difficulty to say which god is meant. And to determine this, he assumes that the term does not come from the Arabic word Ṭâ'ûs, but was occasioned by some "folk-etymology," and that we must look, therefore, for some god-name which resembles the word Ṭâ'ûs. Taking this as a startingpoint, the critic calls attention to the fact that in Fihrist, p. 322, l. 27f, which treats of the feasts and gods of the Ḥaranians, we read that the god Tauz had a feast in middle of Tammuz. He infers from this that the god Tauz is identical with Melek Ṭâ'ûs. And to the question who this god Tauz is, he answers it is Tammuz. To justify his explanation, the writer contends that the Yezidis speak in Kurdish, and according to Justi's *Kurdische Grammatik,* p. 82ff, the change of meem to waw in this language is frequent.[2]

However plausible this process may seem to be, philologically it cannot here yield a satisfactory conclusion. For it is based on wrong premises. It is not true that the word Ṭâ'ûs signifies an ancient deity. It denotes the devil and nothing else. This is so clear to the Yezidis, or to anyone acquainted with their religion, as to leave no need for further discussion. And to question the religious consciousness of a sect is to engage in pure seculation. Likewise, the method of determining this supposed god by the name of some deity resembling it is objectionable. There are many such names. One might also infer that the sect worship Christ under the form of the devil. This theory has actually been advanced.—*Theatre de la Turque,* 364. The statement that in Kurdish the letter meem is changed to waw frequently is untenable, if one would set it up as a grammatical rule to explain such phenomena. What is more, the Kurds pronounce the name tammuz, and nothing else, unless some one has a physiological difficulty which will not permit him to close his lips, so that instead of saying tammuz, he would mutter taouz. The following are a few of many instances to show that meem is not changed to waw in Kurdish ,even in words of Arabic origin: 'Amelie ṣaliḥ (good works), zamanie aḫerat (the last day), the well of Zamsam, Mohammed, and Mustafa (the chosen one), when applied to the prophet, Melek (king), when applied to Ṭâ'ûs. Further the assumption that Ṭâ'ûs does not come from the Arabic Ṭâ'ûs is unverifiable. Unquestionably the attempt to trace this term to tauz, then to Tammuz, was suggested to Professor Lidzbarṣki by the fact that ammuz was the name of an ancient Babylonian god, and that Abu Sayyid Wahb ibn Ibrahim, quoted by an-Nedim, an Arab author of the tenth century, states that the god Tauz has a feast in his honor on the fifteenth of Tammuz (*Fihrist*, p. 322). But according to the author of "*Die Sabier und Sabismus*" (p. 202) the original form of this word is unknown.

Not only the inference which identifies Ṭâ'ûs with Tammuz is based on wrong premises; but, in the Yezidi conception of Melek Ṭâ'ûs, there are no traces of the notion which is held respecting Tammuz. The latter was originally a sun-god, and son of Ea and the goddess Sirdu, and the bridegroom of the goddess Ištar. The legendary poems of Babylonia described him as a shepherd, cut off in the beauty of youth, or slain by the boar's tusk in winter, and mourned for long and vainly by the goddess Ištar. The god Tammuz made his way to Canaan, Cyprus, and thence to Greece. "He had ceased to be the young and beautiful sun-god, and had become the representative of the vegetation of spring, growing by the side of the canals of Babylonia, but parched and destroyed by the fierce heat of the summer. Hence in Babylonia his funeral festival came to be observed in the month of June, and in Palestine two months later. Tammuz had changed his character in passing from country to country, but the idea of him as a slain god, and of his festival as the idealization of human sorrow, a kind of "All Souls Day," was never altered wherever he was adored."[3] Such beliefs are not found in the Yezidi view of their King Peacock. On the contrary his festival is for them the occasion of joy and pleasure.

I conclude, then, that Ṭâ'ûs is the Arabic word meaning peacock, just as Melek is the Arabic word meaning king or angel. The sect write it, pronounce it, and believe it to be so. The faith of the sect finds expression in the fact that they represent their angel Azazil in the form of the peacock.

It seems to me that the real question is not what Melek Ṭâ'ûs is, but how the devil-god came to be symbolized by the image of a bird. This question finds an answer in the fact that the worship of a bird appears to have been the most ancient of idolatry. It is condemned especially in Deut. 4: 16, 17: "Lest ye corrupt yourselves and make a graven image, the similitude of any figure, the likeness of any winged fowl that flieth in the air." And Layard, in his *Nineveh and Its Remains*, vol. II, p. 462, gives the sketch of a bird from one of the slabs dug up at Nimrud. He remarks that the Iyuges, or sacred birds, belonged to the Babylonian and probably also to the Assyrian religion. They were a kind of demons, who exercised a peculiar influence over mankind, resembling the feroher of Zoroastrianism. The oracles attributed to Zoroaster describe them as powers anointed by God.

Their images, made of gold, were in the palace of the king of Babylonia. According to Philostratus they were connected with magic. In Palestine the dove was sacred for the Phoenicians and Philistines. The Jews brought accusation against the Samaritans that they were worshippers of the dove. Sacred doves were found also at Mecca. Nasar (eagle) was a deity of the tribe of Ḥamyar.[4]

A question suggesting itself is how the Yezidi god came to be designated by the form of a peacock. This bird is a native of Ceylon, and not of Mesopotamia or Kurdistan where the Yezidis live.[5] The answer may be found in the Muslim tradition[6] that when the first parents forfeited heaven for eating wheat, they were cast down upon earth. Eve descended upon 'Arafat; Adam at Ceylon; the peacock at Gabul, and Satan at Bilbays. In this myth the devil and the peacock are figured as sharing the same penalty at the same time. According to Surah 2,

28–31, the crime of the former was pride, but nothing is said about the guilt of the latter. We learn, however, from other sources, that the bird in question is thought of as a symbol of pride. In his article "Peacock," in the Enc. Brit., vol. 18, p. 443, Professor A. Newton says: "The bird is well known as the proverbial presonification of pride. It is seldom kept in large numbers for it has a bad reputation for doing mischief in gardens." Hence we may infer that the notion of the peacock as a symbol of pride together with the Koranic idea of Satan's sin led to the formation of the myth; that this story was current among the followers of Yezid bn Unaisa; and that, under the influence of the devil-worshippers of Persia the old tradition lost its original significance, and came to be understood to represent the peacock as a symbol of the god-devil.

Among the three branches of the deity in the second degree, Melek Ṭâ'ûs holds an important place in the theology of the Yezidis. The language used in his praise is so elevated that one is led to think that he is identical with God. Some scholars deny this theory on the ground that the principal prayer of these people is directed to God and no mention is made of King Peacock. Hence they contend also that no direct worship is offered to the latter deity.[7] It seems to me that such a contention is not justifiable. In the first place, the people themselves confess their loyalty to the chief angels. Moreover, the expression in this prayer, "Thou hast neither feather, nor wings, nor arms, nor voice" (see p. 74) is more applicable to the symbol Peacock than to God. There can be no doubt, I think, that in the conception of the sect 'Azazil appears to be identical with God. This fact finds definite expression in the Book of Jilwah. In Chapter I he is represented as being from eternity to eternity, as having absolute control of the world, as being omnipresent and omnipotent and unchangeable. In Chapter II he is said to appear in divers manners to the faithful ones; and life and death are determined by him. And in Chapter III he is declared to be the source of revelation. While this is true, there are other phrases which refer to Ṭā'ūs is being inferior to the great God, but superior to all other gods. He was created, and is under the command of God; but he is made the chief of all.

It is not quite easy to understand the underlying idea in worshipping the devil. Some[8] explain this by supposing he is so bad that he requires constant propitiation; otherwise he will take revenge and cause great misery. For this reason, it is claimed,[9] they do not worship God, because he is so good that he cannot but forgive. This is the usual interpretation, and it is confirmed by the nature of the religious service rendered. It seems to partake much more of a propitiatory than of a eucharistic character, not as the natural expression of love but of fear. This reminds us at once of the Babylonian religion. According to this religion, when any misfortune overtook the worshippers, they regarded it as a sign that their deity was angry, and had therefore left them to their own resources or had become their enemy. To be thus deserted was accounted a calamity because of the innumerable dangers to which the soul was exposed from the action of the powers seen and unseen. So that as a matter of precaution, it was well to maintain a propitiatory attitude. Hence the great object of worship was to secure and retain the somewhat capricious favor of the deity.[10] This is in accord with the natural feeling of man in his primitive state, which leads him rather to dread punishment for his sin than to be thankful for blessings received.

Others[11] hold that the Devil-worshippers believe that their Lord is a fallen angel, now suffering a temporary punishment for his rebellion against the divine will because he deceived Adam, or because he did not recognize the superiority of Adam as commanded by God. But it is not for man to interfere in the relations of God with his angels, whether they be fallen or not; on the contrary man's duty is to venerate them all alike. The great God will be finally reconciled to Ṭâ'ûs, and will restore him to his high place in the celestial hierarchy.

Still others[12] assert that the sect does not believe in an evil spirit but as a true divinity. This theory is not generally accepted, but seems more probable than the preceding ones. For there is nothing in the sacred book to indicate that Melek Ṭâ'ûs is an evil spirit or a fallen angel. On the contrary the charge that he was rejected and driven from heaven is repudiated.

The mentioning of his name is looked upon as an insult to and blasphemy against him because it is based, the Yezidis think, on the assumption that he is degraded. Finally, he is declared to be one of the seven gods, who is now ruling the world for a period of 10,000 years.

It is interesting to note that, in the history of religion, the god of one people is the devil of another In the Avesta, the evil spirits are called daeva (Persian Div); the Aryans of India, in common with the Romans, Celts, and Slavs gave the name of dev (devin, divine, divny) to their good or god-like spirits. Asura is a deity in the Rig Veda, and an evil spirit only in later Brahman theology. Zoroaster thought that the beings whom his opponents worshipped as gods, under the name of daeva, were in reality powers by whom mankind are unwittingly led to their destruction. "In Islam the gods of heathenism are degraded into jinn, just as the gods of north semitic heathenism are called šĕirim (hairy demons) in Lev. 17: 7, or as the gods of Greece and Rome became devils to the early Christians."[18]

The Yezidis' veneration for the devil in their assemblies is paid to his symbol, the sanjak. It is the figure of a peacock with a swelling breast, diminutive head, and widespread tail. The body is full but the tail is flat and fluted. This figure is fixed on the top of a candlestick around which two lamps are placed, one above the other, and containing seven burners. The stand has a bag, and is taken to pieces when carried from place to place. Close by the stand they put water jugs filled with water, to be drunk as a charm by the sick and afflicted. They set the sanjaḳ at the end of a room and cover it with a cloth. Underneath is a plate to receive the contributions. The ḳawwal (sacred musician) kisses the corner of the cloth when he uncovers Melek-Ṭâ'ûs. At a given signal, all arise, then each approaches the sanjaḳ, bows before it and puts his contribution into the plate. On returning to their places, they bow to the image several times and strike their breasts as a token of their desire to propitiate the evil principle.

The Yezidis have seven sanjaḳs, but the Fariḳ (Lieut.-Gen. of the Turkish Army), who tried to convert them to Mohammedanism in 1892, took five of them. Some deny, however, that they were real ones; they say they were imitations. Each sanjaḳ is given a special place in the Emir's palace, where it is furnished with a small brazen bed and a vessel in the form of a mortar placed before it. They burn candles and incense before it day and night. Each sanjaḳ is assigned a special district, the name of which is written on a piece of paper and placed on its shoulder. On the shoulder of the first the district of Šeiḫan, which comprises the villages around Mosul, is indicated; on the second Jabal Sinjar; in the third the district of Halitiyah, which is one of the dependencies of Diarbeker; on the fourth the district of Ḫawariyah, *i. e.*, the Koçhers; on the fifth the district of Malliah, the villages around Aleppo; on the sixth

the district of Sarḥidar, which is in Russia; and the
seventh remains at the tomb of Ŝeiḫ 'Adi.

When sent from village to village of its respective
district, a sanjak is put in a hagibah[14] (saddle-bag)
and carried on a horse that belongs to a pir (religious
teacher). On nearing a certain place, a messenger is
sent to announce in Kurdish "Sanjak hat," "the
Sanjak has come." Then all the people don their
fineries and go out to welcome it with tambourines.
As the representative of Melek Ṭâ'ûs reaches the
town, the pir cries out in Kurdish language, "Sanjak
mevan ki sawa?" (literally: "Whose guest shall the
sanjak be?"). On hearing this, each person makes
a bid for the privilege of entertaining it. Finally he
who bids the highest receives the image. At that
moment the accompanying pir takes the hagibah off
the horse's back and hangs it on the neck of the
person who is to keep the symbol of the devil over
night.

The Yezidis say, that in spite of the frequent wars
and massacres to which the sect has been exposed,
and the plunder and murder of the priests during
their journeys, no Melek Ṭâ'ûs has ever fallen into
the hands of the Mohammedans. When a kawwal
sees danger ahead of him, he buries the Melek Ṭâ'ûs
and afterwards comes himself, or sends some one to
dig up the brazen peacock, and carries it forward in
safety.

Besides revering the devil by adoring his symbol,
the Yezidis venerate him by speaking with great

respect of his name. They refer to him as Melek Ṭā'ûs, King Peacock, or Melek al-Ḳawwat, the Mighty King. They never mention his name; and any allusion to it by others so irritates and vexes them that they put to death persons who have intentionally outraged their feelings by its use. They carefully avoid every expression that resembles in sound the name of Satan. In speaking of shatt (river) they use the common Kurdish word Ave, or the Arabic ma (water). In speaking of the Euphrates, they call it Ave 'Azim, or ma al-kabir, *i. e.*, the great river, or simply al-Fraṭ.

2. Šeiḫ 'Adî

Next to the devil in rank comes Šeiḫ 'Adi. But he is not the historical person whose biography is given by the Mohammedan authors. He is identified with deity and looked upon as a second person in a divine trinity. He is sent by Melek Ṭā'ûs to teach and to warn his chosen people lest they go astray. He is conceived to be everywhere, to be greater than Christ; and, like Melek-Ṣedek, has neither father nor mother. He has not died and will never die. In verse ten of the poems in his praise, he is distinctly said to be the only God. His name is associated with all the myth that human imagination can possibly create about a deity. To express the Yezidi dogma in terms of Christian formula, Šeiḫ 'Adi is the Holy Spirit, who dwells in their prophets, who are called kochaks. He also reveals to them truth and the mysteries of heaven.

The entertaining of such views has led some modern critics to think 'Adi the good and Melek Ṭâ'ûs the evil principle. In the poem (30-32), he is represented as the good deity and the source of all good. Others identify him with Adde or Adi, a disciple of Manes or Mani. Still others regard his name as one of the names of the deity. In this case, his tomb is a myth and the prefix "Šeiḫ" is added to deceive the Mohammedans, and thus to prevent them from desecrating the sacred shrine, just as the Christians call Mar Mattie, Sheikh Mattie, and the convent of Mar Behnan, ḫuder Elias.[15] But the most ingenious theory is that advanced by the Rev. G. P. Badger. He queries whether "the Yezidi 'Adi be not cognate with the Hebrew Ad, the two first letters in the original of Adonai, the Lord, and its compounds, Adonijah, Adonibezek. The writer is aware, however, that "This derivative is open to objection on the ground that the Yezidis write the word with 'ain and not with alif." But he explains: "They write so only in Arabic, of which they know but very little, and not in their own language (Kurdish) in which they do not write it at all. Moreover, they may have assimilated the mode of expressing the title of their deity in bygone days to that of 'Adi, one of the descendants of the Merawian Califs, with whom, from fear of being persecuted by the Mohammedans, they sometimes identified him." Having thus expounded his own view, this English scholar proceeds to repudiate the suggestion that Šeiḫ 'Adi "is the same Adi," one of the disciples of Mani, since there is no proof, according to him, that Mani himself was deified by his followers.

So far as the application of the method of comparative philology is concerned, Badger's theory is more reasonable and tenable than that of Lidzbarski, who, by the same method, attempts to identify Melek Ṭâ'ûs with Tammuz. Nevertheless, the inference of the former is beyond any possible justification. For such a starting-point is misleading when it is not supported by historical proof. A failure to support it thus cannot be regarded as other than deficiency in treatment. Now, while one may be misguided by the Yezidi myth surrounding the personality of Šeiḫ 'Adi, the critical mind can find much in it to aid him in his efforts to discover the true identity of the man. In verse fifty of his poem, for our critic draws his conclusions in the light of this poem, the Šeiḫ receives his authority from God who is his lord; in verse fifty-seven he is a man, 'Adi of Damascus, son of Musafir; in verse eighty he declares that the high place which he had attained is attainable by all who, like him, shall find the truth. To justify my criticism, I need only ask the reader to recall the description by the Mohammedan biographers of the person in question.

The Yezidis offer their worship to Šeiḫ 'Adi, usually when they assemble at his shrine. This is his tomb within a temple. The latter lies in a narrow valley which has only one outlet, as the rock rises on all sides except where a small stream forces its way into a large valley beyond. The tomb stands in a courtyard, and is surrounded by a few buildings in which the guardians and the servants of the sanctuary live. In the vicinity are scattered a number of shacks, each named after a šeiḫ, and supposed to be his tomb. Toward sunset these sacred places are illuminated by burning sesame oil lamps, putting one at the entrance to each tomb in token of their respect; the light lasts but a short time. There are also a few edifices, each belonging to a Yezidi district, in which the pilgrims reside during the time of the feast; so that each portion of the valley is known by the name of the country of those who resort thither. On the lintel of the doorway of the temple, various symbols are engraved,—a lion, a snake, a hatchet, a man and a comb.[26] Their mystical meaning is unknown. They are regarded as mere ornaments placed there at the request of those who furnished money for building the temple. The interior of the temple is made up of an oblong apartment which is divided into three compartments, and a large hall in the centre which is divided by a row of columns; and arches support the roof. To the right of the entrance are a platform, and a spring of water coming from the rock. The latter is regarded with great veneration, and is believed to be derived from the holy well of Zamzam at Mecca. It is used for the baptism of children and for other sacred purposes. Close by there are two small apartments in which are tombs of the saints and of some inferior personage. In the principal halls a few lamps are usually burning, and at sunset lights are scattered over the walls.

The tomb of Šeiḫ 'Adi lies in the inner room, which is dimly lighted. The tomb has a large square cover, upon which is written Ayat al-Kursi, that is, the verse of the throne, which is the 256th verse of surat-al-Baḳarah, or Chapter II of the Koran.

"God. There is no God but He, the Living, the Abiding. Neither slumber nor sleep seizeth Him. To Him belongeth whatsoever is in heaven and whatsoever is on earth. Who is he that can intercede with Him but by His own permission? He knoweth what has been before them and what shall be after them; yet naught of His knowledge do they comprehend, save what he willeth to reveal. His throne reacheth over the heavens and the earth, and the upholding of both burdeneth Him not. He is the High, the Great."

It is related (in the Mishkat, Book IV, 1. 19, Part III) that 'Ali heard Mohammed say in the pulpit, "That person who repeats the Ayat al-Kursi after every prayer shall in no wise be prevented from entering into Paradise, except by life; and whoever says it when he goes to his bedchamber will be kept by God in safety together with his house and the house of his negihbor." Šeiḫ 'Adi might have been in the habit of repeating this verse; and this, perhaps, led to its inscription on the tomb.

In the center of the inner room, close by the tomb,

there is a square plaster case, in which are small balls of clay taken from the tomb. These are sold or distributed to the pilgrims, and regarded as sacred relics, useful against disease and evil spirits. It is said that there are three hundred and sixty lamps in the shrine of 'Adi, which are lit every night. The whole valley in which the shrine lies is held sacred. No impure thing is permitted within its holy bounds. No other than the high priest and the chiefs of the sect are buried near the tomb. Many pilgrims take off their shoes on approaching it, and go barefooted as long as they remain in its vicinity.

Such is the sanctuary of 'Adi, where they offer him their homage. Their worship may be divided into two kinds, direct and indirect. The former consists of traditional hymns sung by the ḳawwals, the sacred musicians of the sect. They are chanted to the sound of flutes and tambourines. The tunes are monotonous and generally loud and harsh. The latter kind consists in celebrating their religious rites with great rejoicing on the feast day of their great saint. And their Ḳubla, the place to which they look while performing their holy ceremonies, is that part of the heaven in which the sun rises.

The great feast of Šeiḫ 'Adi is held yearly on April fifteenth to twentieth, Roman calendar, when the Yezidis from all their districts come to attend the festival celebration. Before entering the valley, men and women perform their ablutions, for no one can enter the sacred valley without having first purified his body and his clothes. The people of the villages are gathered and start together, forming a long procession, preceded by musicians, who play the tambourine and the pipe. They load the donkeys with necessary carpets and domestic utensils. While marching they discharge their guns into the air and sing their war cry. As soon as they see the tower of the tomb, they all together discharge their arms.

The šeiẖs and the principal members of the priesthood are dressed in pure white linen, and all are venerable men with long beards. Only the chief and the ḳawwals and two of the order of the priesthood enter the inner court of the temple, and they always go in barefooted. They start an hour after sunset.[17] The ceremony begins with the exhibition of the holy symbol of Melek Ṭâ'ûs to the priests. No stranger is allowed to witness this ceremony or to know the nature of it. This being done, they begin the rite. The ḳawwals stand against the wall on one side of the court and commences a chant. Some play on the flute, others on the tambourine; and they follow the measure with their voices. The šeiẖs and the chiefs form a procession, walking two by two; the chief priest walks ahead. A faḳir holds in one hand a lighted torch, and in another a large vessel of oil, from which he pours into the lamp from time to time. All are in white apparel except the faḳirs, who are dressed in black. As they walk in a circle, they sing in honor of Šeiẖ 'Adi. Afterward, they sing in honor of 'Isa (Jesus). As they proceed the excitement increases, the chants quicken, the tambourines are beaten more frequently, the faḳirs move faster, the women make tahlil with a great shouting, and the ceremony comes to an end with great noise and excitement. When the chanting is ended, those who were marching in procession kiss, as they pass by, the right side of the temple entrance, where the serpent is figured on the wall. Then the emir stands at this entrance to receive the homage of the šeiḫs and elders who kiss his hand. Afterward all that are present give one another the kiss of peace.[18] After the ceremony the young men and women dance in the outer court until early in the morning.

In the morning the šeiḫs and the ḳawwals offer a short prayer in the temple without any ceremony and some kiss the holy places in the vicinity. When they end, they take the green [19] cover of the tomb of Šeiḫ 'Adi and march with it around the outer court with music. The people rush to them and reverently kiss the corner of the cloth, offering money.

After taking the cover back to its place, the chiefs and priests sit around the inner court. Kochaks at this time bring food and call the people to eat of the hospitality of Šeiḫ 'Adi.[20] After they have finished their meal, a collection is taken for the support of the temple and tomb of their saint. All people that come to the annual festival bring dishes as offerings to their living šeiḫ. After he has indicated his acceptance of them by tasting, these are given to the servants of the sanctuary. When the feast comes to an end, the people return to their several abodes.

(3.) Yezid

The third essential element in the religion of the devil-worshippers is the belief that their sect has taken its origin from Yezid, whom frequently they call God and regard as their ancestral father, to whom they trace their descent. No other worship is offered him. He is given, however, a place of honor in the court of the temple, where, on one side, there is the inscription "Melek Yezid, the mercy of God be upon him"; on the other side "Šeiḫ 'Adî, the mercy of God be upon him." In the corner of this court a lamp is kept burning all night in honor of the two.

NOTES ON CHAPTER II

[1] P. Anastase: *Al-Mašrik,* vol. II, p. 151; Bedrus Efendi Ar-Riḍwani, his letter to A. N. Andrus, April 2, 1887.

[2] Lidzbarski Z. D. N. G., vol. LI, p. 592; he is followed by Makas *Kurdische Studien,* p. 35.

[3] See "Tammuz" in Jastrow's religion of Babylonia and Assyria, and Cheney's Dictionary of the Bible.

[4] R. W. Smith: *Religion of the Semites,* p. 219; Aš-Šahrastanî, vol. II, p. 434. Yakut (vol. IV, p. 780) says: Originally nasr was worshipped by the people of Noah, and from them was brought to the tribe of Hamyar. According to the Syriac doctrine of Addai (Ed. George Philips, p. 24) the people of Edessa worshipped "the eagle as the Arabians."

[5] So far as I am aware no writer on the Yezidis has ever raised this question.

[6] Hughes: *Dictionary of Islam,* p. 21.

[7] Victor *Dingelstedt,* SGM, vol. XIV.

[8] Badger: *The Nestorians,* vol. I, p. 125; Layard, Nineveh, vol. I, p. 297.

[9] P. Anastase: *Al-Mašrik,* vol. II, p. 152.

[10] The Hibbert Journal, vol. V, No. 2, Jan., 1907, p. 337.

[11] Layard: Ibid; *Victor Dingelstedt,* Ibid, p. 299.

[12] Dingelstedt: Ibid.

[13] R. W. Smith: *Religion of the Semites,* p. 120; Fihrist, p. 322, 326, calls the gods of the Harranians devils.

[14] *Hagibah* is a Turkish word, meaning a saddle-back.

[15] Badger: Ibid, p. 247. (137) Ibid, p. 112.

Mr. Badger seems to contend that the Kurdish-speaking people do not pronounce the letter 'ain. This is not true, the Kurds pronounce this letter as well as other gutterals. They sometimes even change the Arabic Alif to ain. This is to be said, however, that in some localities the 'ain is pronounced alif, just as the kaf is changed to alif, but this is not confined to the Kurds, such changes are made by the Arabic- and the Syriac-speaking people also.

[16] The figures of the bull and of the serpent, or of the bull and of the lion were placed at the right and left of the palaces of the Assyrian kings to protect their path. Layard, Nineveh and Babylon, p. 162; Nineveh, vol. II, p. 315; B. F. Harper, Assyrian and Babylonian Literature, pp. 139, 148, 153. The lion was both an ornament and support in the throne of Solomon, Layard, Nineveh, vol. II, p. 301. The hatchet was among the weapons of those who fought in chariots, and carried in the quiver, with the arrows and short angular bow, Nineveh, vol. II, p. 343.

[17] The Mandeans, the star-worshippers, also begin their rasta ceremony after the sunset, and continue it through the night.—*London Standard,* October 19, 1994, Al-Mutaktataf, 23, 88.

[18] The kiss of the peace is a regular part of the church service in the East.

[19] In Mohammedanism, green is the color of šeihs.

[20] This is a communal meal.

CHAPTER III

Other Deities and Festivals

I

The So-Called Seven Divinities

Besides their great saint, the Yezidis believe in seven other šeiḫs through whose intermediation they invoke God. These are also deified and assigned places of honor at Šeiḫ 'Adi's side. In their case as in that of their chief, the tradition has led some critics to believe that they are archangels; others, different attributes of God; and still others, the seven Amshaps of Zoroaster, or immortal spirits of the Avesta. The last conjecture is made by Victor Dingelstadt.[1] Cholsohn goes a step further in making the assertion, "Der Tempel des sheikh Shams ist ohne allen Zweifel ein sonnentempel der so gebaut ist, dass die ernsten Strahlen der sonne so hàufig als möglich auf ihn fallen." The ground for this positive statement is, we are told "Layard berichtet."[2] Now, the English scholar seems to base his contention on the fact that the building is called the sanctuary of Šeiḫ Šams; that the herd of white oxen which are slain on great festivals at Šeiḫ 'Adi's are dedicated to Šams; "that the dedication of the bull to the sun" was generally recognized in the religious system of the ancients, which probably originated in Assyria; and that the Yezidis may have unconsciously preserved a myth of their ancestors.[3] To my mind the ground for such a view is the apriori assumption that the religion of the devil-worshippers is the remnant of an ancient cult, and that every phenomenon in it is to be regarded, therefore, a survival of the past system. For certain reasons I hold that such is not the case.

One reason, as Badger rightly remarks, the Yezidis so designate the place for the sake of brevity, is the entablature over the doorway records the name in full, "Sheikh Shams Ali Beg and Faris." Two persons are mentioned in the inscription.[4] In like manner, the word Šams frequently enters into the construction of Mohammedan names. The most celebrated one that bore this name was Šams u-d-Din of Tabriz, the friend and spiritual guide of Jalal ad-Din, who flourished during the first half of the 13th century of our era.

Moreover, round about the tomb of Šeiḫ 'Adi are many such abandoned shrines, each of which is dedicated to a similar deified šeiḫ. Many of these šeiḫs are known to be historical personages. Take for example, Šeiḫ 'Abd al-Ḳadir of Gilan. He is Šeiḫ Muḥiyyu d Din 'Abd al Ḳadir of Gilan in Persia, the founder of the Ḳadiri order of dervishes. He was born in A. H. 471 (A. D. 1078-9) and died

A. H. 516 (A. D. 1164-5). So also Šeiḫ Kaḍib al-Ban. He was from Mosul, and was a contemporary of Šeiḫ 'Adi. In giving the life of Muḥi ad Din aš-Šharnozuri, Ibn Ḫallikan (v. 2,651) says, "His corpse was removed to a mausoleum built for its reception outside the Maidan Gate of Mosul, near the tomb of Ḳadib al-Ban, the celebrated worker of miracles." Further, Manṣur al-Ḥallaj was a celebrated mystic, revered as a saint by the more advanced sufis. He was put to death with great cruelty at Bagdad in A. H. 309 (A. D. 921–2) on a charge of heresy and blasphemy, because he had said in one of his ecstacies, "Ana-l-Ḥaḳḳ, I am the truth, God." All biographers of sufi saints speak of him with admiration.

There are still others who are mentioned even among the seven šeiḫs enumerated in the principal prayer. Šeiḫ Ḥasan (written also Šeiḫisin) was from Baṣrah. He was a celebrated theologian and died in A. D. 728. His life is given by Ibn Ḫallikan. He was noted for self-mortification, fear of God and devotion. And Faḫr ad-Din is ibn Abd Allah Mohammed Ibn Amar al-Ḥaṣain Ibn al-Ḥasan, Ibn 'Ali Al-Taim al-Bakri al-Taberstani ar-kai-zi (native of Kai in Tabarestan), surnamed Faḫr ad-Din (glory of faith). He was a doctor of the Shafite sect, a pearl of his age, a man without a peer. He surpassed all his contemporaries in scholastic theology, and preached both in Arabic and Persian. He would draw floods of tears from his eyes. His virtues and merits were boundless. He was born at Kai, 25th of

Ramadan, A. H. 54D (A. D. 1150), and died at Herat, the first of Shawal, A. H. 606 (March A. D. 1210) (See ibn Hallikan in loco.)

In the light of these facts, I conclude, then, that those who cannot be identified—for many bear the same name, and we do not know which is which—are also historical personages.

This is what I mean by the statement that in order to yield satisfactory results the inductive method must be supported by historical investigations.

In a question like this, however, the philosophical method also, when carried on critically, may yield a satisfactory result. Accordingly, observations should be made in the sphere of religious consciousness. Now one of the characteristics of the human mind is the tendency to defy man. This is shown in the titles which men gave to their superiors. In the Tell-al-Amarna tablets, we find various kinglets of Syria, in writing to the king of Egypt, address him as "my gods" (ilani-ia). Thus Abimilki of Tyre writes: "To my lord, the king, my son, my god." What is more, a superhuman character is attributed to the dead. This appears from the attitude which the primitive mind entertained towards the deceased. At first, the relation to the dead was hostile, hence their spirits were feared. Gradually, the relation became familiar, so that their association was sought and sacrifices and gifts were offered to them. They came to be looked upon as elohim, who knew the future events. Thus we find that in the Old Testament, worship was offered to the dead, and that the tombs of ancestors and heroes frequently appear as places of worship, as, *e. g.*, the grave of Miriam at Kadish (Num. 26: 1), Even to-day tombs of saints are common in Arabia, and thousands of people visit them annually to ask the intercession of the saints. Likewise, the Nuṣairiyeh of Syria have deified 'Ali, the Drus their chief Hakim, the Babis their Beha, and the Christians their saints.[5] We cannot, therefore, be surprised that the Yezidis have defined their šeiḫs and heroes. They have only shown that common trait of the mind—the tendency to deify man.

It is to be noticed, further, that in the historical development of religions we find that when the stage of the mere belief in spirits is past, individual deities stand out from the great mass of the spirits, and these are plainly imagined to be personal gods, such as Astarte and Ba'al by the side of Hadad and Aschirat.[6] Now this is practically what we find in the evolution of modern Yezidism. Out of many šeiḫs and murids, seven, next to šeiḫ 'Adi, stand out as individual divities.

Yearly festivals in honor of these šeiḫs are commemorated in April at different villages with the same rites as those observed at Šeiḫ 'Adi's tomb. Lamps are nightly lighted and left to burn in the shacks called after the names of their respective šeiḫs; and in those to which a room is attached, ḳawwals assemble at sunset every Tuesday and Thursday, when they burn incense over each tomb; and after watching a short time, and smoking their pipes, they return home.

An interesting festival is that of Šeiḫ Mohammed, celebrated by the people of Ba'šiḳa, where his tomb exists. They say that they are solemnizing the nuptials of Šeiḫ Mohammed, whom they believe to be married once a year. The men and women dance together while the ḳawwals play on their flutes and tambourines. They bring Melek Ṭâ'ûs in procession from Baḥazanie to Ba'šiḳa amid rejoicing and sound of music. Two pirs precede the bearer of the sacred peacock, carrying in their hands lighted candles which they move to and fro. As they pass along the bystanders bow in adoration and, immersing their hands in the smoke, perfume with it their arms and faces. They carry the image of Melek Ṭâ'ûs to the house of the one who is the highest bidder for the honor of entertaining it. Here it remains two days, during which all profane festivals are suspended and visits are paid to it.

II

The Day of Sarsal

In addition to the festivals mentioned above is the one observed on New Year's day, the first Wednesday in April. On this day, the Yezidis say, no drums are to be beaten, for God sits on the throne, holding a conference at which he decrees the events of the year. They also stick wild scarlet anemones to the entrance of their houses. The refraining from the sound of instruments of pleasure on the part of orientals signifies a state of contrition. Hence, it is very likely that the Yezidis entertain the view that on this day God is decreeing their destiny for the coming year; that they must now, therefore, adjust their relation to him with sincere sorrow for sin. If this is so, the significance of the hanging of the flowers at the entrance of their houses can be taken as intended to propitiate the Evil Principle, and to ward off calamity during the coming year. Such a belief has a parallel in many religions. According to Babylonian mythology human destiny was decreed on New Year's day and sealed on the tenth day thereafter. It was therefore necessary to placate the deity, or at least to make sure of one's relation to him, before this particular day. The New Year period was held, therefore, to be of special importance because of the bearing on individual welfare by reason of the good or the evil decision of the gods. Our modern custom of wishing our friends a Happy New Year has perhaps some connection with this idea.[1]

The Day of Atonement (Lev. 23: 27; 25: 29) had a most important place in the Jewish ecclesiastical year. This was the occasion of a thorough purification of the whole nation and of every individual member thereof in their relation to Yahweh. It was designed to deepen afresh the national and individual sense of sin and dread of the judgment of God. According to Talmud (Mišna, Roš hašana, vol. I, 2)

Roš hašana is the most important judgment day, on which all creatures pass for judgment before the Creator. On this day, three books are opened wherein the fate of the wicked, the righteous and those of the intermediate class are recorded. Hence prayer and works of repentance are performed on the New Year from the first to the tenth that an unfavorable decision might be averted (Jewish Ency., art. Penitential Day). R. Akiba says: "On New Year Day all men are judged; and the degree is sealed on the Day of Atonement (Ibid, art. Day of Judgment).

Moreover, the red lilies of the doors of the Yezidis remind us at once of the blood sprinkled on the doorposts of the dwellings of the Israelites in Egypt as a sign for the Destroying Angel to pass over. This notion is found also in a similar practice among the Parsees of India, who hang a string of leaves across the entrances to their houses at the beginning of every new year.

In the light of what has been said, the Yezidis' idea in giving food to the poor at the grave on the day of Sarsal (New Year day), is to propitiate God on behalf of the dead, who are, according to their belief, reincarnated in some form or other.[6]

NOTES ON CHAPTER III

[1] S. G. M., ibid.

[2] *Die Sabien*, I, 296.

[3] *Nineveh and Its Remains*, vol. II, p. 239.

[4] *Nestorians and Their Rituals*, vol. I, p. 117.

[5] S. J. Curtis: *Primitive Semitic Religion To-day*, p. 96; J. A. O. S., vol. 8, 223.

[6] Cf. Marti's *Die Religion des A. T.*, pp. 28–29.

[7] The Hibbert Journal, ibid.

[8] For different interpretation of the Yezidi New Year, see Brockelmann in Z. D. M. G., vol. 55, p. 388.

CHAPTER IV

Sacraments, Religious Observances and Sacerdotal System

I

Sacraments

Circumcision, the Eucharist and baptism are the three religious rites administered by the followers of Yezid. The first rite is optional. But with baptism the case is different; it is a matter of obligation. When a child is born near enough to the tomb of Šeiḫ 'Adi to be taken there without great inconvenience or danger, it should be baptized as early as possible after birth. The ḳawwals in their periodical visitations carry a bottle or skin filled with holy water to baptize those children who cannot be brought to the shrine. The mode of baptism is as follows: A šeiḫ carries the baby into the water, takes off his clothes, and immerses him three times. After the second time, putting his hand on the child's head, he mutters, "Hol hola soultanie Azid, tou bouia berḫe Aizd, saraka rea Azid." ("Hol hola!" Yezid is a sultan. Thou hast become a lamb of Yezid; thou mayest be a martyr for the religion of Yezid.") The parents are not admitted to the domed shack of the spring; they remain outside. The šeiḫ is paid for his services by the father of the child. If the baby be a male, the gift must be more valuable than if it be a female.

Within twenty days from the time of baptism, a male child is circumcised. To perform the rite, two šeiḫs are employed. One holds the child in his lap, the other performs the operation. Before starting, he asks the child to say: "As berḫe Azide Sarum." ("I am the lamb of illuminating Yezid.") If he be too small to repeat, the šeiḫ who holds him repeats the sentence for him. All this is done in the presence of the parents, the relatives and the friends, amid rejoicing with the sound of the flute and the tambourine. When the ceremony is ended, the father of the child entertains all those present for seven successive days, during which period they dance, sing and eat the food sent to them by the friends and neighbors of the circumcised child. When this comes to an end, the two šeiḫs are presented with gifts. Then every one returns home. The reason why they observe the two rites, they say, is that if one does not work the other may, and neither is harmful.

As to the Eucharist,[2] its observance is local. It is usually administered by the Yezidis of a place called Ḫalitiyeh, a dependency of Diarbeker. It is observed in the following manner: They sit around a table. The chief among them holding a ĉup of wine, asks in Kurdish, "Ave Chia." ("What is this?") Then he himself answers, "Ave Kasie 'Isaya." ("This is the cup of Jesus.") He continues, "Ave 'Isa naf rounishtiya." ("Jesus is sitting and present in it.") Having first partaken himself, he passes the cup around. The last person drinks all that is left in the cup.

There is another sacrament among the Yezidis. I refer to the rite of repentance. When persons quarrel, the guilty one, covering his face with his hands, betakes himself to the most venerable šeiẖ to confess his sin. The latter, giving the penitent instructions, enjoins him to kiss the hands of his enemy and those of the members of the priesthood. This having been done, if still no reconciliation be effected, the offending person, whoever he may be, must undergo again the same exercises. When peace is established, the penitent one slaughters a sheep and offers wine to the reconciled one and the clerical body. This rite of repentance, however, is not obligatory.[3]

II

Some Other Religious Practices

Fasting is one of the religious observances. It is kept for three successive days in the month of December, when they profess to commemorate the death of Yezid. Some observe also the forty days' fast in the spring of the year, when the Eastern Christians celebrate the memory of Christ's abstinence from food at the time of his temptation in the wilderness. One person in a family may fast for the rest. During this period fasters abstain from animal food. The chief

Šeiḫ fasts rigidly one month in the year, eating only once in twenty-four hours and immediately after sunset.

Prayer is not considered a religious duty. They never pray; they do not even have a form of prayer, and acknowledge that they do not pray. It is said that when Šeiḫ 'Adi came from Mecca, he told his followers in one of his sermons: "God commanded me to tell you that there is no need of prayer; believe in the power of Melek Ṭâ'ûs and ye shall be saved." They have, however, what is called morning recital, which the devout among them mutters in Kurdish as he rises up from his bed. It is as follows:

"Chand-il-manhatie sobayaka rošh halatie. Hatna mesarmen dou jaladie, meskino raba. Beda šade šada dina mine eik Allah melek šeih-sin Habib Allah makḷub al-mergie ṣalaḥ makḷub w-mergie al-jem's ṣalaḥ Al-bani ma-ieh al-jem'sieh wal jot ḳuobaieh Kwa-šamsi Tauris wal-Fahra-Dinn, washeiḳho Pir. Kawata deira sor, hanpouteka deira chankulie wa-Kabri Zaman wa-ahro douni, Amin."[1]

"How often two executioners came upon me as the morning sun arose. O poor man, stand up and bear witness! Witness for my religion. God is one; the angel Šeiḫ 'Adi and upon his congregation; upon the great shack and the shack of Šeiḫ Tauris and Faḫr ad-Din and to every šeiḫ and pîr, and the power of Deir Zor and Deir Chankalie (two Christian monasteries), and the grave of time (mysterious power), and the Last Day."

III

The Sacerdotal Orders

The hierarchical orders of the Yezidi sect are four. The head šeiḫ is the patriarch of the sect. He directs all the religious affairs of the community and leads them in their rites. He is also the principal interpreter of their religion, the chief spiritual judge, a sacred person, whose hearth is regarded as a sanctuary, only second in importance to Šeiḫ 'Adi's temple, and whose will must be obeyed. His powerful weapon is excommunication. He presides over a tribunal composed of ecclesiastical superiors, which has jurisdiction in religious offences, in questions relating to marriage, and in disputes between the clergy. His charge is hereditary, in direct succession; but if his eldest son be considered unworthy, he may appoint another to succeed him. He is said to be descended from Šeiḫ 'Adi, and is believed to be endowed with supernatural power for healing diseases, and for blessing cattle and crops. Twice a year he visits the neighboring villages to collect contributions, and sends his ḳawwals to far distant districts for the same purpose. Occasionally he takes part in celebrating the marriage of persons of distinction in his community. He is also at times solicited to preside over funeral rites, which are generally conducted by the ḳawwals and šeiḫs. The chief šeiḫ wears a black turban and white garments.

Besides the head šeiḫ, the Yezidis have many other šeiḫs. Each has a parish to look after. Twice a year he visits his parishioners to receive their free-will offerings. If a member of a congregation does not satisfy his šeiḫ, he is anathematized by his spiritual leader, and no one will speak to him or eat with him. Every one of these šeiḫs is supposed to possess a special power, such as the power to drive scorpions away by praying over water and sprinkling it in the corners of the house. They have one called Šeiḫ Deklie, that is, Šeiḫ of the Cocks. His office is to go from village to village to collect chickens. Several of these šeiḫs always reside at Šeiḫ 'Adi's.

The next in dignity are pirs, from the Persian meaning an old man. They wear red turbans and black garments. Then come the ḳawwals, from the Arabic, meaning one who speaks fluently, an orator. And lastly, the fakirs, from the Arabic poor. These are the lowest order in the Yezidi priesthood. (For the different offices of the last three orders, (see p. 69.)

The clergy of all ranks enjoy particular respect. Their persons and homes are held inviolate. They take precedence at public gatherings. And the šeiḫs and pirs possess the much dreaded power of excommunication.

Besides the above, the Yezidis have a temporal chief, who is called amir. His dignity is also hereditary and confined to one family. He is believed to be a descendant of Yezid. He exercises a secondary authority over the Yezidis. He is a mediator between his sect and the Turkish government. He has the power to cut off any refractory member from the community. He has charge of fifty ḳawwals who try to collect for him at their annual visits to each Yezidi district a certain amount of money. The money received by them is divided into two equal parts, one of which goes to the support of the tomb of Šeiḫ 'Adi, and the second part is divided, one-half being for the amir, the other half being shared equally by the ḳawwals.

The name of the present amir is 'Ali, and he resides in Ba'adrie.

NOTES ON CHAPTER IV

[1] Hol Hola is an interjection, or exclamation, expressing sudden emotion, excitement, or feeling, as "Oh!" "Alas!" "Hurrah!" "Hark!" in English.

[2] P. Anastase: *Al-Mašrik,* vol. II, p. 309.

[3] Ibid, p. 311.

[4] Ibid, p. 313.

CHAPTER V

Their Customs

I

Marriage

The Yezidis are endogamic. They forbid union between the secular and the religious classes, as also within certain degrees of relationship. A šeiḫ's son marries only a šeiḫ's daughter; so pirs' sons, pirs' daughters. A layman cannot marry a šeiḫ's or a pir's daughter, but he may take for a wife a ḳawwal's or a kochak's daughter; and ḳawwals' or kochaks' sons may marry laymen's daughters. But if a layman marries a šeiḫ's or a pir's daughter, he must be killed. Marriage is for life, but it is frequently dissolved, divorce being as easy to obtain among them as among Moslems. When a man wants to get rid of his wife, he simply lets her go. Polygamy is allowed, but usually confined to rich men, who generally have two wives. The number of wives is limited to six, except for the amir. A man must have money or cattle in order to be able to get married. The price is called ḳalam. A respectable girl will not sell herself at a low price. Parents get rich if they have several pretty girls; they are the father's property. The ḳalam, dowry, is usually thirty sheep or goats, or the price of them. The man must give presents to the relatives of his bride, parents, brothers, etc. If a couple love each other and cannot marry because the man has no money to pay his sweetheart's father, then they elope. They usually make arrangements before elopement as to where they will stay for a few weeks to escape detection. Some strong men accompany them when they elope. The father of the girl with his relatives follow. If they catch the fugitives, bloodshed may ensue. But if they succeed in escaping, they return after some time and are then forgiven. According to a Kurdish proverb everything is pardoned the brave.

The couple choose one another. The girl informs her mother that she loves so and so. The latter informs her husband. The father acquaints the father of the young man with the fact. When they agree, and the daughter is given to the young man, his kindred come to the house of the bride's father on an appointed day, and give the girl a ring; then they dance, rejoice all night, play, wrestle, and eat black raisins. After that the young couple are allowed to arrange nuptial meetings in the company of a matron, who is presented with a gift.

When the time of marriage comes, the family of the bridegroom invites the relatives. Each takes with him a silk handkerchief as a present for the bride. For three days they drink "ărak," sing and dance to the sound of flutes and drums at the house of the young man. After that, the women, two by two, ride on horseback together, and likewise the men. The men take with them their children, who ride behind them. In this manner they go to the bride's house, discharging their guns as they proceed. When they reach the house they all discharge their guns together. Hearing the sound, the father comes out and according to the custom, asks the visitors what they want. They respond "Your daughter," all answering at once. Then he goes in and tells his wife. After putting upon their daughter a scarlet ḫailiyah (veil), which covers her from head to foot, they bring her out. Everyone of the children takes a spoon from the bride's house and sticks it in his turban. After being brought to the house of the bridegroom, the bride is kept behind a curtain in the corner of a darkened room for three days, and the young man is not allowed to see her during this period.

On the third day, the bridegroom is sought early in the morning, and led in triumph by his friends from house to house, receiving at each a small present. He is then placed within a circle of dancers, and the guests and bystanders wetting small coins stick them to his forehead. The money is collected as it falls in an open handkerchief held by his companions. After this ceremony a number of the young men, who have attached themselves to the bridegroom, lock the most wealthy of their companions in a dark room until they are willing to pay a ransom for their release. The money thus taken is added to the dowry of the newly married couple.

On the evening of the third day the šeiḫ takes the bridegroom to the bride. Putting the hand of one in that of the other, and covering the couple with a ḫailiyah, he asks the bride, "Who are you?" "I am the daughter of so and so," responds she. Then he asks the bridegroom the same question. After receiving an answer, the šeiḫ asks, "Will you take this young woman as a wife," and "Do you want this young man as a husband?" After hearing each say "Yes," the šeiḫ marks their shoulders and foreheads with red ink, and hands them a stick. As each holds one end of it, he asks them to break it in the middle, leaving one-half in the hand of each. Then the šeiḫ says, "So you remain one until death breaks you asunder."

When this is done, he takes the couple to a room and locks them in, waiting at the door. After a while the bridegroom knocks at the door three times. Understanding the signal, the priest discharges his gun, and all the bystanders outside follow his example. After shouting and dancing for some time, the šeiḫ sends them home. When they first meet, the newly wedded husband strikes his young wife with a small stone as a token of his superiority over her. For seven days, they stay at home and do no work. Now, if the husband dies first, the wife goes to her father's house.

With the Yezidis, the family bonds are stronger than those of the tribe. The family proper consists of parents and their children, married, and unmarried, living in the same house. Respect for parents and elder persons is considered a virtue, as it is among all the eastern people. The head of the family is the sole proprietor of the possessions of the family, and holds full control over his wife and children, who are bound to obey him. Only personal objects and dress are the property of the wife. He can punish his wife and the children. If a son leaves his father's house, he is beyond the father's authority, but not beyond his moral influence. A father is to maintain his family, defend it, and answer charges brought against its members. Next to the father in authority stands the eldest son.

Women are inferior to men; married women must obey their husbands. They work like men; they till the ground, take care of cattle, fight the enemy and are courageous and very independent. This enables the young women to choose their sweethearts and run away with them. They converse with men freely. A woman does not conceal her face unless she is stared at, when she draws a corner of her mantle over her face.

Married women are dressed entirely in white, and their shirt is of the same cut as the man's, with a white herchief under their chin, and another over their heads, held by the 'agal or woollen cord of the Bedouins. The girls wear white skirts and drawers, and over them colored zabouns, long dresses open in front and confined at the waist by a girdle ornamented with pieces of silver. They bind fancy kerchiefs around their heads and adorn themselves with coins as well as with glass and amber beads.

The men wear shirts closed up to the neck, and their religious law forbids them to wear the common eastern shirts open in front. Their shirt is the distinctive mark by which the Yezidi sect is recognized at once. They are clothed besides with loose trousers and cloaks, both of white, and with a black turban, from beneath which their hair falls in ringlets. They usually carry long rifles in their hands, pistols in their girdles, and a sword at their side.

In their physical characteristics they are like the Kurds, wild, rough, uncultured. They are muscular, active, and capable of bearing great hardship. In general, they are a fine, manly race: tall or of medium stature, with large chest; strong deep voice, audible afar; clear, keen eye; frank and confident, or fierce and angry; nose of moderate length, and fairly small head. Their legs are rather short, but the soles of their feet are large. Their complexion is usually dark and their eyes are black. But there are different types. The predominant type is tall, with black hair, fine regular nose, and bluish brown eyes. The rest are of shorter stature, with longer features; light, bright eyes; and large, irregular nose. The Yezidis sometime shave the hair off their head, leaving only a long, thin forelock.

II

Funerals

If a young or well-known man dies, they make in his likeness a wooden form and clothe it in the dead man's clothes. Then the musicians play mourning tunes, while the relatives stand round the model. After wailing for a while, they walk in procession in a circle around the form, and now and then kneel down to receive a blessing from it. Those who come to the scene, according to their custom, ask the parents of the dead man, "What have you?" They reply, "We have the wedding of our son." They continue wailing for three days. Afterward they distribute food on behalf of the dead. For a year they give a plate of food with a loaf of bread daily to some person, thinking that thereby they are feeding their own dead. On the seventh and fortieth day from the time of death, they visit the grave to mourn over their lost one. Now, if the dead be a common man, he is not honored with such a ceremony. He is usually buried an hour or two after his death.

The funeral rites are simple. The body of the Yezidi, like that of a Mohammedan, is washed in running water. After being laid on a flat board, they dress him with his former clothes, close the openings in his body with pieces of cotton, place the sacred clay of Šeiẖ 'Adi in his mouth, on his face and forehead, under his shoulders and eyes, and on his stomach. This done, they carry the dead on the board to the cemetery. The ḳawwals, burning incense, lead the procession; the immediate relatives, especially the women, following, dressed in white and throwing dust over their heads, and accompanied by male and female friends and neighbors. If the dead be a man, they then dance, the mother or the wife holding in one hand the sword or shield of the dead, and in the other, long locks cut from her own hair. They bury him with his face turned toward the north star. Everyone present throws a little dust over the grave while saying, "O man, thou wert dust and hast returned to dust to-day." Then the šeiḫ says, "When we say, 'Let us rise and go home,' then the dead man will say, 'I will not go home with the people.' And when he tries to get up, his head will strike the stone, when he will say, 'O, I am among the dead.'" When they return home, the family slaughters oxen and sheep and gives meat to the poor. The poor kill four or five sheep; the rich, a hundred. The kochaks prophesy of the dead, whether he will return to the earth or will go to another world.

They hold that some will be eternally condemned, but that all will spend an expiatory period; and that the dead have communion with the living, in which the good souls dwelling in the heavens make revelations to their brethren on earth.

III

Nationality

Four different theories have been advanced as to the race to which the Yezidis belong. There are those who think them to be of Indo-European origin, for there is a type among them that has a white skin, a round skull, blue eyes and light hair. And there are those who suppose them to be Arabs on the ground that the color of skin of another type is brown, their eyes are wide, their lips are thick and their hair is dark. The western writers, moreover, have in the past always taken them for Kurds because of the close resemblance of the two in appearance and manners. In his "La Turquie d'Asie," Vitol Cunet says that though the Yezidis have been taken for Kurds, they can no longer be regarded as such, for in many ways they resemble other nationalities. On the other hand Hormuzd Rassam, in his "Asshur and the Land of Nimrud" seems to agree with those who suppose them to be of Assyrian origin. He bases this inference on the independent and martial spirit which they possess, and their tendency to rebel against their oppressors, which, according to him, may be taken as an indication of ancestral inheritance.[1]

IV

Locality

The Yezidis dwell principally in five districts, the most prominent among these being that of Šeiḫan. This term is the Persian plural of šeiḫ, an old man; and it signifies the country where šeiḫs dwell. This district lies northeast of Mosul, covering a wide area in which are many villages. It is their Palestine. In it lies their Mecca, Lalish, where their sacred shrine, the tomb of Šeiḫ 'Adi, is. Lališh is the centre of their national and religious life. It is situated in a deep, picturesque valley. Its slopes are covered with a dense wood, and at the bottom of it runs the sacred water. Other notable places here are the two adjoining villages, Ba'ašika and Baḥazanie, at the foot of the mountain of Rabban Hormuzd, a six hours' ride from Mosul. The former is the center of the tombs of their šeiḫs; the latter is their principal burial place, to which bodies are carried from all the various districts. It was formerly a Christian village with a monastery. And Ba'adrie, northeast of the City of Mosul, about ten hours' ride away, is the village where their amir resides. It is close to Šeiḫ 'Adi's.

Next in importance is Jabal Sinjar. The term "Sinjar" is Persian, meaning a bird, perhaps an eagle. It signifies that its inhabitants are, like the eagle, safe and cannot be caught.[2] Sinjar is about three days' journey from Mosul. It is a solitary range, fifty miles long and nine miles broad, rising in the midst of the desert. From its summit, the eye ranges on one side over the vast level wilderness stretching to the Euphrates, and on the other over the plain bounded by the Tigris and the lofty mountains of Kurdistan. Nisibin and Mardin are both visible in the distance. One can see the hills of Ba'adrie and Šeiḫ 'Adi. Among the sacred places of this district are two villages: Assofa, where two ziarahs are found, and distinguished from afar by their white spires, and Aldina, where one ziarah exists. In almost every Sinjar village, there is to be found a covered water which they use as a fortress during their fights with the Kurds or with the Turkish army. The devil-worshippers of this locality are commonly called Yezidis, while those of Šeiḫan are known both as Yezidis and Dawaseni.

Another district is Ḫalitiyeh, which includes all the territory north and northeast of the Tigris in the province of Diarbeker. The Malliyeh region includes all the territory west of the Euphrates and Aleppo. And the Saraḥdar section includes the Caucasus in southern Russia. Some regard the Lepchos of India also as Yezidis, who, in the early appearance of the sect, went there to proselyte the Hindoos.[3]

V

Dwellings

In regard to their dwellings, the Yezidis are divided into two classes: Ahl al-ḥaḍar, the people of the villages or cultivated land, and Ahl al Wabar, the people of the tents. The villages are built of clay, stone or mud, and unburned brick. A village consists of about sixty houses. A house is divided into three principal rooms, opening one into another. These are separated by a wall about six feet high, upon which are placed wooden pillars supporting the ceiling. The roof rests on trunks of trees raised on rude stones in the centre chamber, which is open on one side to the air. The sides of the room are honeycombed with small recesses like pigeon-holes. The whole is plastered with white plaster, fancy designs in red being introduced here and there. The houses are kept neat and clean. They say that cleanliness is next to heaven.

Now, the people of the tents are, like the Arab Bedouins, nomadic, having no houses and no permanent place of abode. They form but a small portion of the Yezidis, and are called Kotchar.

VI

The Language

The language of the Yezidis, in common with the Kurds, is Kurdish, which belongs to the Iranian group of the Indo-European or Indo-Germanic stock. This Kurmanji possesses a number of dialects not differing much from one another, except the zaza dialect, which is spoken in eastern Mesopotamia by the Kurds, called Ali Alla. The main characteristic of the Kurmangi are the great brevity of its words and the simplicity of its grammatical forms. It is fairly rich in vowels, and richer in deep gutteral sounds. Though Kurdish is the general language of the Yezidis, their religious mysteries are in Arabic. Both languages are spoken by those living in the Sinjar hills and in Šeiḫan.

VII

Occupation

Generally speaking, the Yezidis are an industrious people, but they do not engage in business. This is due to their belief that any form of business leads to cheating and lying, and hence to cursing Melek-Ṭâ'ûs, *i. e.*, the devil. Their usual occupation is agriculture and cattle-raising. The Yezidis of Sinjar, who constitute almost the entire population, raise fruit, such as figs and grapes; also almonds and nuts. Jabal Sinjar is famous for its figs. Those who live in the Russian territory, like the sweeper class of India, are mainly engaged in menial work. But those in the districts of Redwan and Midyat are given to house-breaking and highway robbery; they are the terror of those regions.

The Yezidis seldom appear in the cities; and when they do they conceal their peculiarities as much as possible, for the Christians and Mohammedans are wont to seek amusement at their expense. When they find a Yezidi in their company, they draw a circle about him on the ground, from which he superstitiously believes he cannot get out, until some one breaks it. They annoy him by crying out, Na'lat Šaitan, *i. e.,* Satan be cursed. Moreover, city people keep aloof from the habitations of these despised devil-worshippers. Accordingly the Yezidis have little intercourse with their neighbors.

NOTES ON CHAPTER V

[1] In his letter to me, of date August 6, 1907, the Rev. A. N. Andrus, of Mardin, expresses the opinion that "many of the Yezidis around Sinjar might have come from Indian stock" on the ground that "they are darker and more lithe than the Kurds around them."

[2] P. Anastase: *Al-Mašrik*, vol. II, p. 831.

[3] Cf. *Al-Mašrik*, vol. II, p. 734.

CHAPTER VI

List of the Yezidi Tribes

(The materials were collected for me by A. N. Andrus, of Mardin)

The Tribes Across the River From Mosul

1 The tribe named Šeiḫan lives in the mountains of Al-Ḳôš, and has sixteen villages. They are all under the orders of Šeiḫ 'Alî Beg Paša, the Amir, or chief of the Yezidis. This tribe can furnish 1,600 guns for war. Said 'Alî Paša has received from the Turkish government the order of Amir ul-Umara "the Amir of Amirs." He has a brother who has received the order of Miry Miran, "the Amirs of Amirs." He has a second brother who has received the order of Romeli Beglar Begi, "the Beg of Begs." These three are all sons of the former Amir Husein Beg.

2 The Denôdi tribe lives in Dakoke district. It occupies fifteen villages, and can bring 800 guns to war.

3 The Howari tribe lives in the region of Zaḫo. This tribe is nomadic, lives in tents, and can furnish 200 guns for war. It has two chiefs, Bedri Sohr and Dar Bazi Ḥusein. They are all shepherds.

The Tribes at Sinjar and Jezireh Districts

Tribes.	Tents.	Villages.	Guns.	Population.	District.
Aldaghi		1	100	500	Sinjar
Bekura		1	100	500	
Chalka		1	100	500	
Dalka		1	100	500	
Fakir		1	100	500	
Gabara		2	150	650	
Haska		1	200	1,000	
Hubaba		6	900	4,500	
Jabri		1	50	250	
Jovana		6	500	2,000	
Kiran		2	600	3,000	
Menduka		2	300	1,500	
Mihrka		2	200	1,000	
Sumoka		6	1,200	6,000	
Uleki		1	70	350	
		34	4,570		
Amoad	400	...	400	2,000	Alkoš
Dunadi	...	15	800	4,800	Duhok
Havveri	100	...	100	500	Zaho
Shekan	...	16	1,200	7,200	Alkoš
Rashukan	150	...	150	750	Jezireh
Samukie	...	6	500	2,500	Midyat
Sohranie	...	15	300	1,500	
Grand total	650	86	8,020	42,000	

The Tribes of Midyat Region, Usually Called Jabal Tor Al-'Abedin (Mountain of the Worshipers)

This region lies one day's journey east of Mardin. There are three tribes here.

1 The tribe of Šemmike. This tribe inhabits six villages and can produce, when needed, 500 guns.

2 The tribe called Soḥrani. There are fifteen small villages to this tribe with 300 guns. These all have houses built of stone, and till the ground.

3 The tribe called Mamila. This tribe has seven villages:

Mazazah, Bajinne, Kochano, Keuṅos, Taka, Harobia, and Namirdani.

Mr. Andrus writes me that he has learned of this tribe from Ḳas Samuel, a Jacobite Syrian priest of Mazazeh near Midyat.

The tribe of Bešreyeh, northwest of Jabal Al-Tor.

There was only one tribe in this district; it was called Ḥaltah. This tribe had five villages:

Reḍwan, Dooshah, Selaḫar, Bimbarik, and Ṣoolân.

On account of the oppression of the government on the one hand, and of the Kurdish tribes around them on the other, this tribe has moved to the Sinjar Mountains.

The tribes around Weran Šahr or Goran Šahr, "the destroyed or the sunken city," because it was destroyed by earthquake or in war. This district lies southwest of Mardin.

1 The Denodi tribe. This is probably an offshoot of the Dahoke tribe of the same name. It occupies three villages, and has Ḥasan Ḳanjo for the chief. He is now the right arm of Ibrahim Paša of the Ḥamideyeh army. The three villages are Salmi, Payamlo and Desi.

2 The tribe called Šerḳiân. This tribe has seven subdivisions:

a. Turnah lives in one village called Laulanji.

b. Ḳupan occupies four villages: (1) Aḫmazut. (2) Nuḳti. (3) Al-Ašeḫan. (4) Ṣhda Ausman.

c. Beleki has six villages: (1) Šahda Nasu. (2) Mouzan Šeiḫ Bersef. (3) Mouzan Auṣo. (4) Menk-šuri Minet. (5) Al-Ḳaureyee. (6) Menmenik.

d. Adi has three villages: (1) Tal Ṭarik. (2) Karmi Apo 'Alo Rešo. (3) Karmi Sim, u, Kor Kahiah. Sim means hoof; u, and; kor, blind; kahiah, head man.

e. Mardanah occupies two villages: (1) Hajj Zain. (2) Ḳara Ḳuzeye.

f. Malla Ḳachar has one village: Malla Kachar means the Malla flees.

g. Maskan occupies two villages: Birj Baluji.

h. Suḥan has one village, Kafar Bali.

CHAPTER VII

PERSECUTION

The history of the Yezidis, like that of the Jews, has been one of persecution. The causes of their misfortune have been (1) the fact that they are not regarded as the people of the Book; and with such the Mohammedans have no treaty, no binding oath, as they do with the other non-Mohammedan bodies. For this reason they have to make choice between conversion and the sword, and it is unlawful even to take taxes from them. Consequently they must accept the faith or be killed. (2) Their ceremonies have given rise among their neighbors to fables confounding their practices with those of the Nuṣairi of Syria and ascribing to them certain midnight orgies, which obtained for them the name of cheraĝ sanderañ, i. e., the extinguishers of light. (3) Their determined refusal to enter the military service. The Yezidis with the Christians have been exempt from the military service on the general law sanctioned by the Koran; namely, that none but true believers can serve in the armies of the state. But from time to time the Turkish government has endeavored to raise recruits for the regular troops among the Yezidis on the ground that, being of no recognized infidel sect, they must be included like the Druses of Mount Lebanon among Mohammedans. But they have resisted the orders, alleging that their religious law absolutely forbids them to take the oath to which the Turkish soldiers are weekly subjected, to wear the blue color and certain portions of the uniform, and to eat several articles of food that are offered to the troops. Hence they have suffered severely at the hands of the local authorities.

One of the most cruel persecutions which the Yezidis have suffered was that brought upon them in the Šeiḫan district by the famous Beg Rawmanduz in 1832, who had united most of the Kurdish tribes of the surrounding mountains under his command. His cry was to crush the hateful sect of the devil-worshipers. The forces of 'Ali Beg, the then amir of the Yezidis, were much inferior in number to those of the Khurdish Beg. The latter (Ali Beg) was defeated, therefore, and fell into the hands of his enemy, who put him to death. The people of Šeiḫan fled to Mosul. It was in the spring and the river had overflowed and carried the bridge away. A few succeeded in crossing, but the greater multitude of men, women and children were left on the opposite side and crowded on tal 'Armus. The hostile Beg followed and butchered them indiscriminately, showing no mercy, while the people of Mosul were witnessing the horrible massacre from the other side of the stream and hearing the cry of the unfortunate for their help, unwilling to render any assistance. For the Christians were helpless and Mohammedans rejoiced to see the devil-worshippers exterminated. From this cruel action of the Beg of Rawanduz, the mounds of Nineveh gained the name "Kuyunjik," *i. e.*, "the slaughter of the sheep."

Soon after this Suleiman Paša of Bagdad sent a large army to Sinjar under the command of Lutfee Effendi, who set fire to the Jabal Sinjar and caused all the inhabitants to flee. Then Ḥafiz Paša of Diarbeker attempted the subjugation of the Yezidis of Sinjar, on the ground that they were plunderers. After meeting some resistance, he accomplished his purpose in 1837, and appointed a Moslem to watch over them. At another time Mohammed Rašid Pasha of Mosul attacked Sinjar. On both occasions there was a massacre. The Yezidis took refuge in caves, where they were either suffocated by smoke or killed by the discharge of cannon. And thus the population was reduced by three-fourths. These and other similar injustices at the hands of the Pašas of Bagdad and Mosul and the Kurdish chiefs led the Yezidis from time to time to send a deputation to lay their grievances before the agents of the European powers, and they have even sent commissioners to the Sultan. They finally succeeded in enlisting the interest of Lord Stratford in 1847 to obtain at Constantinople a proper recognition of their religion and exemption from military service.

But the severest of all persecutions, to which I was an eye-witness, was perhaps the one which the Yezidis of both Šeiḫan and Sinjar suffered in 1892 at the hands of Fariḳ 'Omar Paša, Lieutenant-General of the Turkish Army. This Fariḳ was sent in the summer of 1892 as a special commissioner by the Sultan to accomplish certain definite things in the states of Mosul and Bagdad: to collect twenty years' unpaid taxes; to induce the Bedouins to exchange their nomadic life for village life; to convert the Yezidis of Šeiḫan and Jabal Sinjar from their idolatry to the true faith. He was a harsh man in his manners and methods. He first invited some of their chiefs to Mosul. They came and listened to what the new Paša had to say. They met him when Mijlis al-Edarah, council of the state, composed of 'Olama and a few Christians, was in session. In the presence of these noblemen he began to tell them that if they would give up their devil-worship, they would be rewarded with high place and rank, and would please the great Allah. But they answered not. When the Fariḳ saw that his words failed to persuade them, he began to apply the weapon of cruelty. He cast them into prison; some died; others fled; and a few, through the fear of torture and painful death, pronounced al-šehâdah[2] with their lips but not from their hearts. Then he sent an army to their villages, and commanded them to choose between Islam and the sword. 'Omar Beg, his son, who was commanding the soldiers, directed them to slaughter the men, and take captives the pretty women and girls and marry them. He slew about five hundred men. Many became

Moslems from fear, among these Merza Beg, their civil chief.

Then he placed mullas among them to teach the children the Muslim faith, and ordered the newly converted Yezidis to pray five times every day and to perform all the religious rites. To make them continue to be Mohammedans, he tore down their shrines, especially those at Baḥzanie and Baašiḳa. Such events encouraged the Kurds to come down and add greater cruelty to what was already done.

But amir 'Ali Beg, their chief in civil and religious affairs, after long imprisonment and torture, did not change his religious belief. That he might not be an example of firmness to the Yezidis, the Fariḳ banished him with soldiers to Katamuni, a place near Constantinople.

As a consequence of these persecutions, the number of the Yezidis has been considerably decreased. In the fifteenth century there were 250,000. At the beginning of the nineteenth century there were 200,000. Thy are still declining and remaining under the clouds of misconception, and are consequently objects of aversion and hatred. But they console themselves with the idea that they suffer in the cause of their religious convictions.

NOTES ON CHAPTER VII

[1] Cherog sonderan is Turkish; sonderan is the participle of the infinitive of to put out, and cherag, literally lamp, is the object of sonderan. In Turkish the object precedes the verb; cf. Yani sarfi Otamani "the New Turkish Grammar" (in the Turkish language, ed. Ahmad Jaudat & Co., Constantinople, 1318 A. H.), p. 77.

[2] Kalimatu, š-Šehâdah is as follows: "I testify that there is no deity but God and that Mohammed is apostle of God."

BIBLIOGRAPHY

THIS PAGE LEFT BLANK BY ORIGINAL PUBLISHER, USE FOR NOTES

BIBLIOGRAPHY

Arabic

A manuscript containing the Sacred Book of the Yezidis and their tranditions.

Two other manuscripts containing the history of the Yezidis.

Aš-Šahrastani: Kitab Al-Milal wa, n-Niḥal (ed. Wm. Eureton, London, MDCCCXLIII, vol. 1, p. 101 seq).

Yasin Al-Ḫatib Al 'Omari Al-Mauṣili: Al Der al Maknûn fi-l-Miâṯer Al-Maḍiyat min Al-Ḳerûn, "Šeiḫ 'Adi."

Mohammed Al-'Omari Al-Mausili: Manhal-al-Uliya wa Masrab ul Asfiya, "Šeiḫ 'Adi."

Ibn Ḫallikan: Wafaiyat-el-'Aiyan (Cairo A. H. 1310, A. D. 1894), vol. 1, p. 316.

Fihrist: ed Flügel: The Religion of Ḥauran, p. 190 seq.

Yakout: Lališ. Vol. IV, p. 373.

Abu-l-Ḳasim Ibn Ḥauḳal: Kitab Al-Masalik Wal-Mamalik (ed. M. J. De Goeje, 1873, Lyden) Hakkari, p. 144.

Anistase: Al-Mašriḳ, vol. II.

Tabari on Sabeans: The Sixth Session of the Oriental Congress. Leide, 1883, pp. 300-340.

Syriac

A manuscript containing an abstract about the History of the Yezidis.

Kurdish

Yezidis Songs and Prayers, in manuscript.

Turkish

Vital Cunet: Translation of *La Turquie d'Asie*, Constantinople.

Turkish Reader (Constantinople, A. H. 1318), Second Part, p. 20 seq.

English

G. P. Badger: *The Nestorians and Their Rituals*, vol. I.

Layard: *Nineveh and Its Remains*, vol. II.

Layard: *Nineveh and Babylon*.

Ainsworth: *Travels and Researches in Asia Minor*.

H. Southgate: *A Tour Through Armenia, Persia, and Mesopotamia*, vol. II.

J. B. Fraser: *Mesopotamia and Persia*.

G. J. Rich: *Residence in Kurdistan*, vol. II, 1836.

Fletcher: *Notes From Nineveh*, 1850.

F. Parrot: *Journey to Ararat*.

J. S. Buckingham: *Travels in Assyria, Media, and Persia*.

F. Millingen: *Wild Life Among the Kurds*, 1870.

Hormuzd Rassam: *Asshur and the Land of Nimrod.*

O. F. Pary: *Six Months in a Syrian Monastery.*

F. D. Green: *The Armenian Crisis in Turkey.*

A. V. Williams Jackson: *Persia, Past and Present.*

A. V. Williams Jackson: J. A. O. S., 25, 178 seq.

A. V. Williams Jackson: The Article, "Yezidis," in New Inter. Enc., vol. 17, p. 939.

Victor Dingelstedt: Scottish Geog. Mag., vol. 14, p. 295.

Ainsworth: *Transactions of the Ethnographical Society*, vol. 1, 1861.

Forbes: J. R. G. Sc., vol. LX, p. 409; *Account of Yezidis of Jabal Sinjar.*

Tylor: Journal of Geographical Society, 1868.

Hextheusen: Transcaucasia: *Account of Yezidis in Russia.*

Ainsworth: *Travels and Researches in Asia Minor*, Ch. XXXI.

Transactions of the Syro-Egyptian Society, 1855, the article, "Yezidis."

A. N. Andrus: Missionary Ency. Art. "Yezidis."

The Independent, January 17, 1895.

R. Gottheil: *Mandeans* in J. U. Cycl.

R. Gottheil: *Sabeans* in J. U. Cycl.

K. Kessler: *Mandeans*, Enc. Brit.

E. H. Bunbury: *Sabeans*, Enc. Brit.

T. H. Hughes: Muslin Sect, in Dict. of Islam.

French

J. Menant: *Les Yezidis.*

Niebuhr: *Voyage en Arabie,* 1776.

Olivier: *Voyage dans l'Empire Othoman,* T. 2, p. 342.

Ernest Chantre: *Le Tour du Monde, de Beyrouth a Tiflis,* p. 184.

Nuchel Febore: *Theatre de la Turque, Paris, 1682.*

Vital Cunet: *La Turquie d'Asie,* p. 772.

Eugene Bore: Dict. des Religions, T. IV, Yezidis.

Eugene Bore: *Correspondence d'Orient,* T. I, p. 401; T. II, pp. 188, 272.

Siouffi: Journal Asiatique, 1885, p. 78, and 1882, p. 252.

J. B. Chabot: Journal Asiatique, 1896, p. 100.

M. Tcheraz: *Le Museon,* T. LX No. 2, p. 194.

M. Garzoni: *Sylvestre de Sacy,* 1809, pp. 105, 191.

E. Reclus: Nouvelle Geographie, T. LX, p. 432.

Spiro: Bulletin Soc. Neuchatel Geog., Tome 12, p. 275.

Annales des Rois d'Assyria, sall II, No. 39.

Receu du Monde Musulman, August, 1908.

German

Schwolsohn: *Dies Sabien,* vol. II, p. 201.

Hugo Makas: *Kurdische Studien,* p. 35.

M. Lidzbarski: Z. D. M. G., vol. 51, p. 592.

C. Brockelmann: Z. D. M. G., vol. 55, p. 388.

C. Brockelmann: Z. A., vol. 16, p. 399.
Archie fur Anthropologie, vol. 27, p. 3.
Das Ausland, 50 Jahrgang, No. 39 und 40 Stutgart, 1886, p. 790.

LATIN

Assemani: *Bibliotheca Orientalis, Clementino-Vatican*, vol. III, p. 493.
T. Hyde: *Historia Religionis vetrum Persarum*, 1760.

INDEX

THIS PAGE LEFT BLANK BY ORIGINAL PUBLISHER,
USE FOR NOTES

THIS PAGE LEFT BLANK BY ORIGINAL PUBLISHER, US
FOR NOTES

Joseph, Isya.

Devil worship

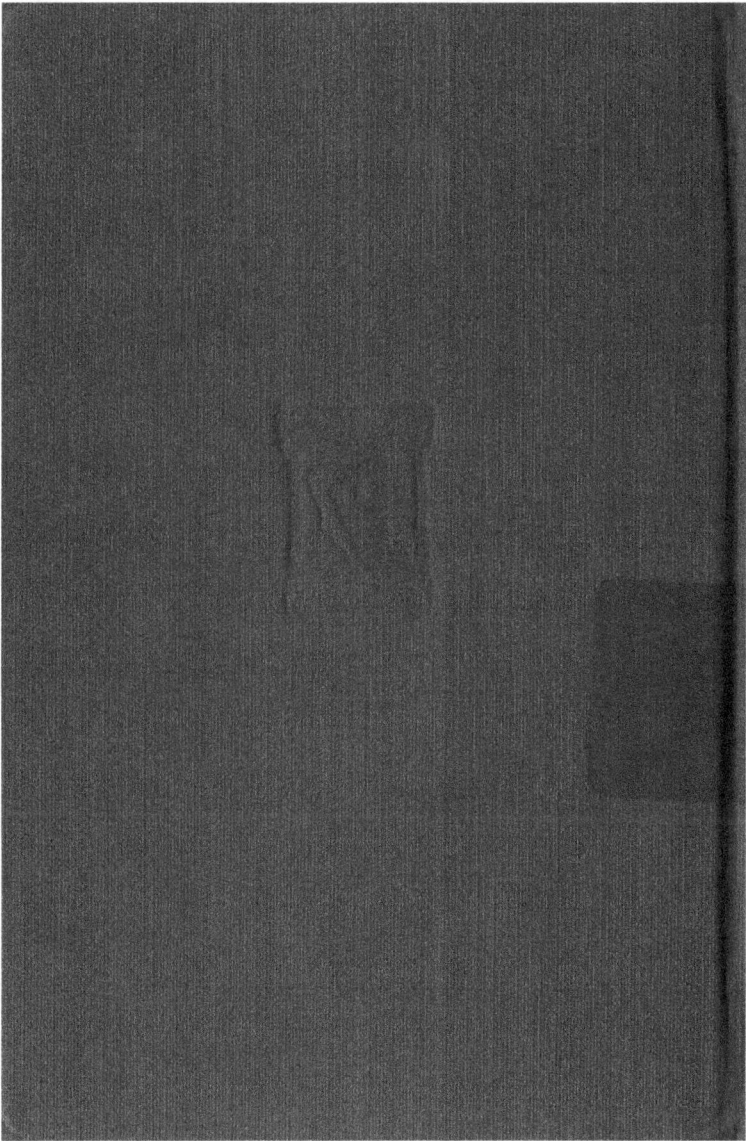

BIO AND BOOK CATALOG

THE SORCERESS CAGLIASTRO

Author, Publisher, Teacher, Designer... Creator of the Science of Sorcery, the foremost authority on Blood Sorcery and Necromancy in the hands of 9......and creator of THE FIRM..... an elite hidden group of Sorcerers working together to produce broad stroke results...

This book is published by

IRON RING PUBLISHING.

The Sorceress owns another publishing company which prints original works of all kinds from other writers as well as the esteemed series

RESCUED KNOWLEDGE PROJECT

…for Publishing info on North Sea Tales visit www.northseatales.com

For more information about The Science of Sorcery or to study with The Sorceress Cagliastro visit www.cagliastrotheironring.com or

Email

sorceresscagliastro@gmail.com

TITLES FROM BOTH OF THE FOLLOWING LISTS CAN BE FOUND AT

amazon.com/author/sorceresscagliastro

TITLES BY IRON RING PUBLISHING

The Science of Sorcery Beginner Course Vol 1 (NECESSARY FOR BEGINNERS)

Blood Sorcery Bible Vol 2 – Striking the Target the Practitioner and the Static Practice (BEST IN THE SERIES)

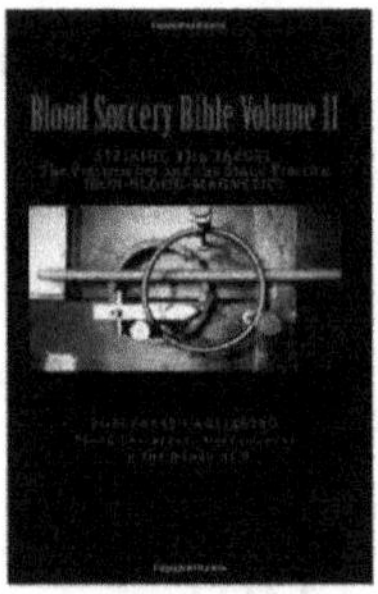

Blood Sorcery Bible Vol 1 – Rituals in Necromancy

Blood Sorcery Bible Vol 1 Workbook

DIVINATION

29 DEADLY Sigils to Harm, Gain Control or Disarm: Developed with THE BOY, a Daemon from the Hockomock Swamp

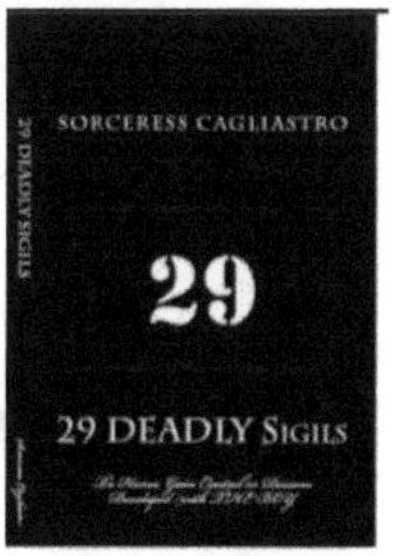

23 Sigils of Selfish Indulgence

25 Sigils, Dark Circles from the Iron Ring

26 Daemons Revisited

26 Daemons Workbook

Flatline Ritual, vengeance through dream interruption

Menstrual Blood and Semen – A Sorcery Manual

Al Vostro Servizio

Al Vostro Servizio Due

TITLES BY NORTH SEA TALES PUBLISHING

LEONA RETURNED – Script

Mini stories of justice: 7 really scary tales and lots of undeserved consequences

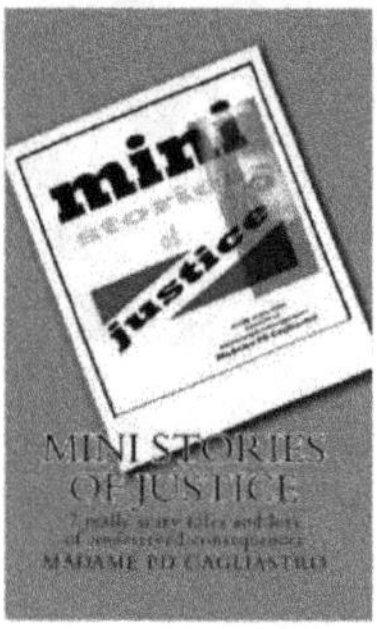

"...and then Minami's baby died..." ORIGINAL BOOK

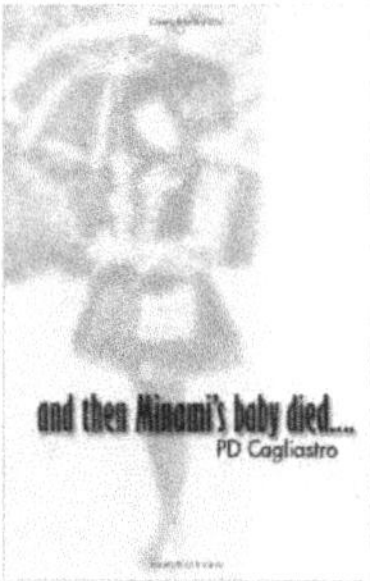

"...and then Minami's baby died..." SCRIPT

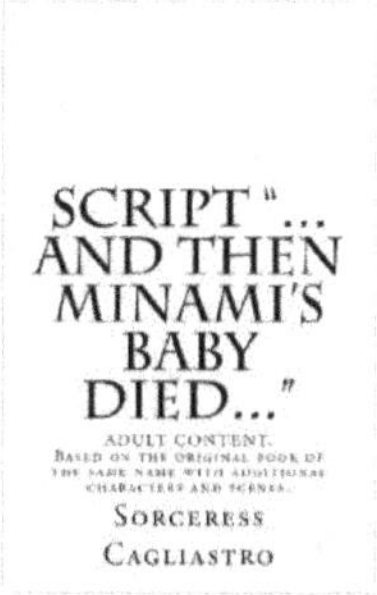

RESCUED KNOWLEDGE PROJECT published by North Sea Tales:

+CREE AND ENGLISH, a primer, originally published 1890

WORLDS FAIR COOK BOOK, originally published 1893

DEALINGS WITH THE DEAD, originally published first in 1856

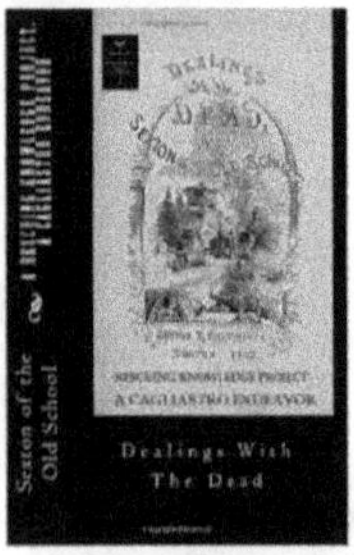

MONEY MAKINGFORMULAS from the National Scientific Laboratories published first in1921

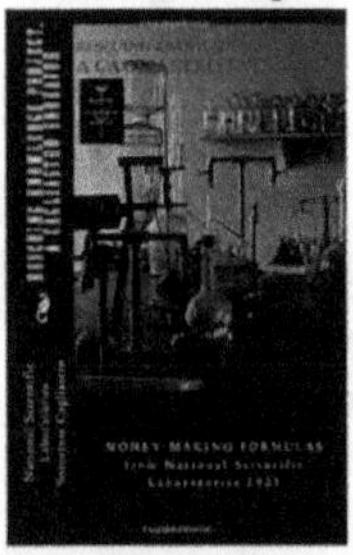

+DEVISES AND EMBLEMS originally published in 1699

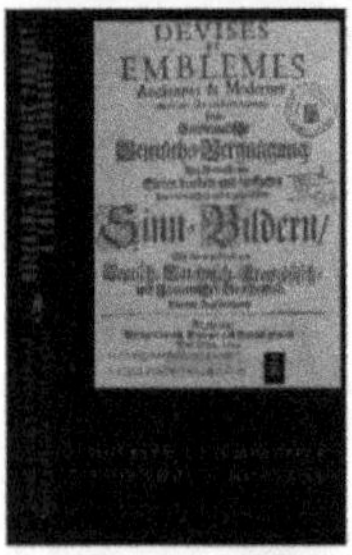

ICE BREAKERS originally published 1819

UPCOMING NOVEL

Collette Mandolino Begins to Cry expected by April 2016

CONTACT INFORMATION

For author information or for submission guidelines for

NORTH SEA TALES PUBLISHING

please visit www.northseatales.com or contact

northseatales440@gmail.com

For your Sorcery Requirements, Readings/Consultations, to become a student of the Science of Sorcery, or for information about

THE FIRM….

sorceresscagliastro@gmail.com

BLANK PAGE FOR NOTES

BLANK PAGE FOR NOTES

BLANK PAGE FOR NOTES

www.ingramcontent.com/pod-product-compliance
Lightning Source LLC
Chambersburg PA
CBHW071736270326
41928CB00013B/2697
* 9 7 8 0 6 9 2 6 2 9 9 4 9 *